The New Choice Effect:

How To Make The Right Decisions Quickly Without Overthinking

Gina Trimarco Klauder

The New Choice Effect:
How To Make The Right Decisions
Quickly Without Overthinking
By Gina Trimarco Klauder

Copyright © 2025 by Gina Trimarco Klauder.
All rights reserved.

Printed in the USA on sustainably harvested paper. No part of this book may be copied or reproduced in any form without express written consent of the publisher and author except in the case of brief quotations embodied in critical articles and reviews.

For information, contact
BDI Publishers, Atlanta, Georgia
bdipublishers@gmail.com

Layout Design: Tudor Maier
BDI Publishers

Atlanta, Georgia

ISBN: 978-1-946637-41-3

Table of Contents

Dedication..5
Foreword..5
Preface..7
    Why This Book Is For You...10
    How To Get The Most Out Of This Book...................12
Introduction..15

Part One: The Art & Science of New Choice...........................17
Chapter 1: Choosing To Pivot With Power..........................19
Chapter 2: Choosing The Improvised Path..........................37
Chapter 3: Choosing To Rewire Your Brain........................47

Part Two: Life-Changing Choices...65
Chapter 4: Choosing To Rewrite Your Learning Journey........67
Chapter 5: Choosing Work That Lights You Up.....................80
Chapter 6: Choosing Financial Truth With Confidence.........92
Chapter 7: Choosing To Create a Healthy Home.................107
Chapter 8: Choosing Family Roles.......................................117
Chapter 9: Choosing Love That Empowers.........................131
Chapter 10: Choosing The Right Circle of Friends..............145
Chapter 11: Choosing To Grow...156
Chapter 12: Choosing How to Heal.....................................171
Chapter 13: Choosing A Spiritual Path................................185
Chapter 14: Choosing Time to Succeed...............................199
Chapter 15: Choosing Purpose & Passion Over Pressure......212
Chapter 16: Choosing The End with Peace..........................228

Part Three: The Perpetual Encore.......................................241
Chapter 17: Choosing To Move Forward -
The Stage Is Always Yours...243

References..249
About the Author..253

DEDICATION

Dedicated to my husband David and my stepson Chase for being the best new choices I've ever made in my life. Thank you for choosing me.

FOREWORD

*By Louis J. Muglia, MD, PhD,
President and CEO, Burroughs Wellcome Fund*

I often ask myself, how can I enhance my creativity and that of those around me? How can I cultivate the ideal workplace? How can I promote equity and justice on this both beautiful and challenged planet? The journey to answer any of these questions rarely follows a linear path. As the old adage goes, if you go from point A to B in a straight line, you probably haven't learned anything along the way. Progress depends on curiosity, on the willingness to ask new questions in new ways, and on the courage and resilience to make a new choice when uncertainty and potential failure exist. That spirit of inquiry, adaptation, and courage is precisely what The New Choice Effect captures so powerfully.

Throughout my career as a physician-scientist studying preterm birth, and now as CEO of a nonprofit foundation advancing biomedical sciences and education, I've learned that understanding complex systems, whether biological, social, or organizational, requires openness to surprise and a willingness to receive feedback without defensiveness. Breakthroughs are motivated by curiosity, a willingness to welcome new ideas, and course adjustments. The moment we allow ourselves to say, "There's another way to see this," we move closer to truth and to progress. Gina Trimarco Klauder's work beautifully bridges that idea into the realms of personal growth, leadership, and communication.

Drawing from improvisational theatre and coaching, Gina offers a practical framework for making thoughtful choices in moments of change. Her approach connects the neuroscience of decision-making with the everyday practice of emphasizing flexibility, empathy, and awareness. Innovation depends on the improvisational principle of "Yes, And," which acknowledges what is known and builds forward from it. The same principle guides the mindset presented in this book. Science, the human spirit behind it, and the actions that science makes possible advance humanity. That same combination of knowledge, spirit, and action is embodied in this book. This mindset fuels both innovation in the lab, in the office, in our communities, and transformation in life.

The New Choice Effect is more than a self-development book. It's an invitation to reimagine how we think, lead, and connect. In a world increasingly defined by complexity and division, Gina reminds us that we always have a choice to empathically listen, to adapt, to respond with purpose rather than fear. That choice, repeated over time, shapes not just our outcomes but our evolution. I believe readers will find in these pages both inspiration and utility: a new lens for viewing their own capacity for growth, resilience, and creativity.

—**Louis J. Muglia, M.D., Ph.D.**
President and CEO, Burroughs Wellcome Fund

PREFACE
Embracing the Power of New Choice

A Life Shaped by Decisions

"Make a Decision, and Then Make It Right" – Abraham Hicks

The quote from Abraham Hicks didn't shake the ground beneath me, but it did settle into my bones. I realized I'd been instinctively living by that mindset most of my life. I'm the kind of person who jumps in, makes the call, and figures it out on the fly. I've made plenty of impulsive decisions. I've overanalyzed others into oblivion. Still, I rarely regret the choices I make, because I know how to pivot, thanks to improv.

If you're not familiar with improv, it's a form of theater where most or all of the performance is unplanned, unscripted or created spontaneously. Improv taught me to move without a script. To stay in motion. To trust myself enough to speak before the sentence is fully formed. Most importantly, improv guided me to choose again when the moment calls for it.

In improv, there's a game we play onstage called "New Choice." Two people start a scene, and at any point, the director can yell "New Choice!" forcing the last person who spoke to immediately revise their line. It might take three, four, or five tries to land something useful or hilarious, but you keep going. You don't freeze. You just respond, shift, and build.

It's fast. It's uncomfortable. And it's magic.

Watching that game one night in my theater, the concept struck me like a divine revelation. I'd been trying to write a book for years. Different titles, different frameworks. All too much or not enough. But in that moment, I saw it clearly: this wasn't just an improv tool. It was a way of life. A way out of analysis paralysis. A mindset shift for anyone stuck, scared, or spiraling.

"New Choice" became the spine of this book.

I've spent the last thirty years applying improvisational principles to leadership, sales, personal growth, and team development. I've coached executives through career reinventions. I've taught burned-out teams how to collaborate again. I've helped people walk through grief, divorce, reinvention, and reintegration. Not because I had all the answers. But because I knew how to help them move.

Movement matters, especially when life doesn't go as planned, which, let's be honest, is most of the time.

My own New Choice moment came in college, when I stared down an accounting degree I never wanted. My dad, practical and proud, saw stability. I saw a spreadsheet-shaped coffin. On a whim, I signed up for an improv class at The Second City in Chicago. That one class gave me something my business classes never could: access to creativity, confidence, and aliveness.

 Looking back now, I'm amazed by how many times improv saved me. The practice helped me leave a toxic job, start a business, end a marriage, and fall in love again. Through improv, I learned to grieve, forgive, and parent myself. Every time I felt stuck or scared, I returned to the basics: Say yes. Stay present. Choose again.

This book is for anyone standing at the edge of something.

Maybe you're done playing small, but unsure how to start fresh. Maybe you're overthinking everything, and it's costing you time, energy, and peace. Maybe you're wildly successful by other people's standards, but something feels off.

You don't need a five-year plan. You need your next choice.

The stories, tools, and exercises in this book are designed to help you move mentally, emotionally, and practically. You'll learn how to interrupt old patterns, get out of your own way, and trust your instincts. You'll learn to pivot without panic. You'll learn to reframe fear as fuel. And you'll do it all using principles grounded in neuroscience, theater, and lived experience.

Acknowledging fear while deciding to act becomes the practice. You're rebuilding how decisions are made in your mind, creating space for clarity and the courage to lead.

You already know what needs to change. You just need the right invitation. This is yours.

Let's begin.

Why This Book is For You

Everything we do boils down to a choice. Some choices flow naturally, such as deciding what to eat for breakfast or how many times to hit the snooze button. Others, though, hold the power to flip your world upside down. A new career, a big move, or a relationship shift can change everything.

While some decisions feel automatic, others can grind us to a screeching halt. Why? Because we are terrified of getting it wrong. This fear is not just about disappointing ourselves. It is also about everyone else's expectations, judgments, and opinions. The fear of making the "wrong" call traps us in our comfort zones. It keeps us stuck, playing small, and sabotages our potential to grow, evolve, and adapt to the inevitable challenges that life presents.

Does this sound like your personal highlight reel? Then this book is for you.

Perhaps you're stuck at a career crossroads, knowing you need a change but hesitant to take the leap. Or maybe you are spinning your wheels in patterns that no longer serve you but cannot figure out how to break free. You might face a huge life decision and worry about making the "wrong" move. Perhaps you are leading others through uncertain times and yearning for tools to make the process less chaotic and more effective. Maybe you're ready for something new, but you're missing the framework to take that first step. Or perhaps you are overthinking everything and finally need a way to trust yourself.

This book has your back, no matter where you are or what you feel stuck on. Here's the game-changer: you are not broken and do not need some perfect decision-making blueprint to appear magically. What you need is a mindset shift. You need a way to look at decisions and change with curiosity instead of fear. That is where improvisational theater's "New Choice" technique comes in.

This is not about snapping your fingers and pretending the fear isn't there. It is about rewiring how you approach decisions, adapting to unexpected changes, and pivoting when life throws you off course. With the tools in this book, you will learn how to stop obsessing over getting it "right" and start taking bold steps forward, whether they are big, small, calculated, or completely spontaneous.

If you are ready to stop second-guessing, shake off decision-making paralysis, and step boldly into the unknown, let's get started. You have already made your first choice by picking up this book. Now let's make the next one together.

You could read this book cover to cover, curl up on the couch with a cup of coffee, and power through it. Or you could dive straight into the chapters that resonate most with your current challenges. Life is messy, time is short, and sometimes you need answers. That is why I designed this book to work for you, no matter where you are in your journey.

Each chapter stands independently while building on the core principles introduced in Part One. This means you can take the scenic route and read straight through or jump to the sections that meet you where you are. Consider this book your trusty sidekick, a tool you can turn to anytime for inspiration, clarity, and a gentle nudge to get moving again.

This book is not about helping you make "perfect" decisions because, spoiler alert, they do not exist. The goal is to help you feel more confident, nimble, and skilled at pivoting when life throws you a curveball. Every "new choice" is a chance to learn, grow, and move closer to the life you are meant to live.

How To Get the Most Out of This Book

1. **Follow the Journey**

   - Begin at the start and work your way through.
   - Build a strong foundation with Part One and deepen your practice chapter by chapter.
   - Let the core frameworks compound for lasting transformation.

2. **Zoom In on What Matters**

   - Use the Table of Contents like a menu.
   - Pinpoint the areas where you feel stuck and dive into those chapters first.
   - Each chapter is self-contained, so you won't miss context if you skip around.

3. **Let the Stories Lead**

   - Start with the personal stories that speak to your own experience.
   - Use the reflection prompts to apply the lessons to your life in real-time.
   - As themes connect, you'll start to see how mindset shifts show up across all areas.

4. **Working with Stories**

The stories are springboards for change. Each one is paired with tools to help you translate insight into action:

- Reflection questions ("Side Coaching") to help you apply the story to your own life
- Journaling prompts to uncover more profound clarity
- Action steps ("Scene Work") to build momentum
- Optional resources if you want to keep going

See The *Script Notes*

Keep an eye out for *Script Notes* throughout the book. These are my real-life summaries of the new choices I made, moments when I rewrote the script in my own story. Each one captures a snapshot of insight, growth, or transformation drawn from experience. Use them as mental reset buttons, reflection tools, or sparks of inspiration when you need a fast mindset shift.

Tips for Deeper Impact:

1. Read the story twice, once for inspiration, once for application

2. Don't rush the prompts. Let them land.

3. Take immediate action, even if it's small

4. Track your growth to notice how your choices evolve

Putting It into Practice

This book is designed for doing, not just thinking.

Start Small

- Begin by calling "New Choice" on one low-stakes decision per day.
- Use morning rituals or daily reflections to check in with your mindset

Share the Experience

- Learning is more effective when it's social. Share your takeaways.
- Join or form a New Choice practice group.
- Use the discussion prompts to go deeper with others.

Keep Moving Forward

- Expect resistance. It's part of the process.
- When you hit a wall, revisit the concepts in Part One.
- See setbacks as signals, not stop signs.

Final Note

Forward movement trumps flawless execution. Stuck? Come back to this book. Allow it to challenge, encourage, and remind you what you're capable of. Keep choosing. Keep shifting. Keep growing.

INTRODUCTION

Thriving Through Fearless Decision-Making

Every moment hinges on a choice. Some choices are simple, like what to eat, when to speak up, and where to sit. Other decisions carry more weight. Should I leave this job, end this relationship, stay safe, or take the leap?

Big decisions can feel like standing at a fork in the road without a map. The pressure builds, overthinking kicks in, and the fear of regret or failure takes over. You stall. You spin. You stay stuck.

Here's the truth: doing nothing is still a choice. And it often costs more than getting it "wrong."

In a world that moves fast and expects certainty, staying stuck is no longer sustainable. Change doesn't care if you're ready. What worked yesterday may not be enough to get you through next week. You need a way to pivot with clarity and courage, without overthinking yourself into a standstill.

Improv comedy gave birth to the principles in this book, but they extend far beyond getting laughs on stage. Improvisation teaches you to trust yourself in real time, to respond instead of reacting, and to build something from nothing. You learn to lead without a script, adapt with intention, and move forward even when the way is unclear.

This book presents a novel approach to decision-making, combining practicality, research-backed insights, and a human perspective. You'll learn to break through the fear that clouds your thinking and build momentum using tools grounded in behavioral science, emotional intelligence, and the mechanics of the brain.

At the core are two principles:

- **New Choice**, an improv game that interrupts default patterns and opens new possibilities

- **Yes, And**, a mindset that helps you stay present, accept what's real, and build from it without judgment

You'll learn why these work, not just in theory, but in your brain. Neuroscience shows how habits, fear responses, and outdated beliefs form pathways that keep us stuck. Improvisation disrupts those patterns. It rewires your thinking by creating safety, flexibility, and space for better choices. Research from Charles Limb, Sara Lazar, and others confirms what performers have long known: creativity, resilience, and adaptability can be trained.

Whether you're navigating a major life transition, leading others through change, or simply tired of overthinking everything, this book is a guide to choosing again with confidence.

The chapters ahead are packed with stories, scripts, tools, and prompts. You'll be invited to explore your defaults, stretch your capacity, and choose a new approach in areas of life that feel foggy, frustrating, or filled with fear.

Getting unstuck matters more than getting it perfect.

No more spinning. No more waiting for permission. You've already made one choice by picking up this book.

Let's make decisions in the moment ... and love it!

Part One
The Art & Science of New Choice

Chapter 1:
Choosing To Pivot With Power

What Happens When You Stop Freezing and Start Choosing Again

"When a scene (or situation) isn't working, you don't need permission to change it.

You just call 'New Choice' and create something better."

– *Gina Trimarco*

The fluorescent lights buzzed overhead as I stood before a room of skeptical executives. They had paid a considerable sum for corporate decision-making training, and here I was, about to make them play a theater game. I could feel their resistance. Arms were crossed, slight eye rolls appeared, and the familiar tension of high-achieving professionals being asked to step outside their comfort zones was evident.

"Let's try something," I said, steadying my voice. "I need two volunteers for a quick demonstration."

After a moment of uncomfortable silence, Sarah, the marketing director, and James, the head of operations, raised their hands reluctantly. As they made their way to the front of the room, I explained the game's rules.

"You're going to role-play a simple scenario. You're discussing the status of the company holiday party. Whenever I call out 'New Choice,' the last person who spoke must immediately change what they just said. The only rule is that you cannot question the change. You must accept it and continue the scene based on the new reality."

Sarah and James exchanged dubious looks but nodded their agreement. The scene began:

Sarah: "What's the plan for the holiday party?" James: "We're not doing it due to budget." Me: "New Choice!"

James: "John said we can't afford it." Sarah: "Well, he's the boss, so it's his call." Me: "New Choice!"

Sarah: "That's terrible. Let's do it anyway." James: "Oh no, but what if he…"

Me: "New Choice!"

James: "Yes, let's do it anyway and ask for forgiveness later!"

By this point, the energy in the room had shifted. Other executives leaned forward, some smiling, while others called out suggestions. What started as a simple theater game revealed something profound about how we approach decisions, instincts, and the process of change.

The Game That Changes Everything

"New Choice" is more than just an improvisational exercise; it is a powerful metaphor for how we can approach decisions in every aspect of our lives. The game works because it eliminates decision paralysis by removing the luxury of overthinking. In the moment, every choice feels temporary, and even mistakes transform into opportunities for learning.

This exercise also builds adaptive confidence. By practicing quick decision-making, you learn to trust your instincts and develop a greater comfort with uncertainty. Each rapid choice reinforces your ability to act decisively, even when the path forward feels unclear.

Perhaps most importantly, "New Choice" transforms your mindset. It helps shift your thinking from rigid to flexible, teaching you to view failure as simply a step in the iterative process. Over time, this reframing creates a sense of psychological safety, making it easier to embrace change and take bold steps forward.

What starts as a game becomes a profound framework for navigating life's challenges with creativity, resilience, and an open mind.

During the training session, I watched as the executives began to embrace this framework. A simple game was helping them think on their feet, reframe challenges, and find creative solutions. However, the magic of "New Choice" extends beyond the exercise itself. It rests on a foundational mindset that drives all improvisation: the "Yes, And" principle.

The "Yes, And" Principle

At the heart of improvisation is the "Yes, And" principle, which essentially means acceptance without judgment. It is a deceptively simple idea with a transformative impact because it focuses on making others look good. "Yes, And" is the opposite of the all-too-common "Yes, but," which throws a wrench into conversations and ideas before they even have a chance to grow.

In every improv scene, performers are taught to accept whatever their scene partner offers ("Yes") and then build on it ("And"). This practice creates a foundation of trust, creativity, and collaboration. Let's break it down:

Say "Yes" to What Is:

The "Yes" part is about acceptance. In improv, this means not rejecting your partner's idea, no matter how absurd it might seem. In life, it means acknowledging the reality of a situation without resistance or denial. Saying "Yes" does not mean you agree with everything or that you must like it. It simply means you are willing to start from where you are.

Add Your "And":

The "And" is where the magic happens. It is about contribution and creativity. Once you have accepted what is in front of you, you heighten it or add to it. You build momentum. You move the story forward.

Together, "Yes, And" becomes a mindset of openness and possibility. It is an antidote to resistance, fear, and overthinking.

Developing the skill of "Yes, And" requires practice and mindfulness. By cultivating an open mind of acceptance without judgment, you will create a mental environment that is primed for adaptability. This mindset allows you to navigate change more effectively, learn from diverse experiences, and innovate in the face of challenges. It is a powerful tool for enhancing your overall capacity for improvised intelligence, actively engaging all three "acts" of your neurological theater.

To begin this cultivation process, let us start with the literal "Yes, And" exercise that every improv student learns on their first day of an improv class. This exercise uses the literal words "Yes, And" as a replacement for the typical English phrase "Yes, but." Before diving into the popular "Yes, And" improv exercise, it is essential to understand the impact "Yes, but" has on our thinking and interactions.

"Yes, but" is a phrase often used in conversation to partially agree with a statement or proposal while also introducing a counterpoint or qualification. It typically signals two things. First, there is acknowledgment, where the speaker recognizes the truth or validity of what was said. Second, there is a reservation, where the speaker expresses doubts, concerns, or raises additional points.

This phrase is often used to soften disagreement, introduce a different perspective, add nuance to a discussion, or transition to a counterargument.

For example:

Person A: "The weather is perfect for a picnic today!"

Person B: "Yes, but the forecast shows it might rain later."

In this case, Person B agrees that the current weather is nice but raises a concern about potential rain.

Here is a business-oriented example:

Person A (Team Member): "Our new product launch exceeded our sales targets by 20% in the first week!"

Person B (Manager): "Yes, but we are seeing a higher-than-expected return rate, which could impact our long-term profitability."

The frequent use of "Yes, but" can sometimes hinder acceptance without judgment or disrupt positive interactions. Shifting to "Yes, and" in conversations fosters more collaborative idea building. The next chapter will explore the impact of using literal "Yes, And" versus "Yes, but" in communication and relationship-building.

Now, let's try the Literal "Yes, And" framework. If you tend to have an analytical mindset, I encourage you to embrace this framework, even if it feels awkward at first. It is especially helpful to practice with others. You will likely not have real-life conversations that exactly mirror this exercise. The purpose is to improve your ability to communicate, validate, and collaborate with others.

Here is an example of a literal "Yes, And" exercise conversation:

Person A (Team Member): "Our new product launch exceeded our sales targets by 20% in the first week!"

Person B (Manager): "Yes, our new product launch exceeded our sales targets by 20% in the first week, and we will need to increase production to keep up with demand."

Person A: "Yes, we will need to increase production to keep up with demand, and this success might allow us to expand into new markets."

Person B: "Yes, this success might allow us to expand into new markets, and we should start preparing our international marketing strategy."

Instructions for the Literal "Yes, And" Exercise:

- Person A starts with a short statement.

- Person B replies with "Yes," repeats what Person A said verbatim, says "And," and adds a new thought as a sentence (not a question).

- Person A replies with "Yes," repeats Person B's addition verbatim, says "And," and adds a new thought as a sentence.

Exercise Rules:

- Keep sentences short for easier verbatim repetition.

- Adjust pronouns for validation (e.g., "I like chocolate" becomes "You like chocolate").

- Only make statements, as questions derail the ability to stay in the moment.

- Do not worry about making sense in your responses.

Practicing the literal "Yes, And" exercise can be transformative in ways that extend far beyond improv games. First, it teaches you to actively listen without constantly thinking ahead to what you want to say next. Instead of rushing to respond, you pause to hear and process what someone else is offering truly.

This practice also encourages you to pause and observe your own initial reactions. Instead of immediately acting on them, you take a moment to reflect. That pause creates space for deeper understanding and intentional responses.

Another benefit is how "Yes, And" fosters a sense of validation in your conversations. When you accept and build on what someone else contributes, you create an atmosphere of understanding. It is not about agreeing with everything but about acknowledging their perspective in a way that makes them feel seen and valued.

This exercise also helps you embrace contributions from others without jumping to immediate criticism. By suspending judgment, you allow creativity and collaboration to flourish.

As you continue practicing, you will notice how it trains you to adapt in real time. You learn to engage in conversations without needing a pre-planned script or focusing on your agenda.

Instead, you stay present, flexible, and open to possibilities.

Finally, "Yes, And" can help you recognize your own biases and how they shape your judgments, which creates awareness of the filters you bring into conversations, helping you to respond with greater empathy and clarity.

Through these small shifts, "Yes, And" becomes a powerful tool for building better communication, deeper connections, and a mindset that thrives on adaptability.

By incorporating these practices, individuals and organizations can enhance their adaptability, creativity, and emotional intelligence. As we shift from "Yes, but" to "Yes, And," we begin rewiring our neural pathways to become more open, flexible, and adaptive. The shift in language and mindset serves as a practical application for strengthening the neural connections associated with adaptability and creative problem-solving. I discuss in more detail in upcoming chapters.

How "Yes, And" Sets the Stage for New Choices

"New Choice" is an improv game where players perform a scene while a facilitator calls out "New Choice" or signals with a horn. When this happens, the player must immediately change their last line or action to a different option. There is no time to hesitate or overthink. The game illustrates the numerous possibilities that exist in any given moment and helps develop a crucial skill: flexibility in decision-making.

This flexibility would not be possible without the "Yes, And" mindset. Without it, we risk shutting down ideas, hesitating, or becoming stuck in a loop of self-doubt. The connection between the two lies in their shared foundation of adaptability. The practice of "Yes, And" teaches us to adjust on the fly and remain open to possibilities, which is critical for thriving in the "New Choice" exercise. It also encourages creativity by shifting our focus away from rejecting ideas to exploring and building on them. This openness to innovation is at the heart of what makes "New Choice" so effective.

Perhaps the most profound link between "Yes, And" and "New Choice" is the momentum it creates. By saying "Yes" to what is and adding to it with "And," we learn to keep moving forward, even when the path is unclear. This forward momentum is essential for navigating the "New Choice" game, where stopping to analyze or overthink would disrupt the flow. Together, these practices build confidence, creativity, and resilience.

The "New Choice" exercise develops what I like to call "choice flexibility." It shows us that every moment holds multiple possibilities and that our first choice is not always the best one. Adaptation becomes a natural and necessary part of growth. Through quick changes, we discover that being stuck is often a choice we make, and breaking free creates space for new outcomes.

The exercise reinforces that innovation often arises from necessity and that change is not just inevitable but full of opportunity.

This framework ultimately teaches us how to remain flexible and creative when circumstances shift. It is a skill that has applications in both personal and professional life, where the ability to adapt can make all the difference.

Breaking Free from Default Patterns

Think about how many of your daily decisions are made on autopilot. You probably take the same route to work, eat at the same lunch spot, or respond to familiar situations in predictable ways. These default choices are not necessarily bad. They help conserve mental energy for more urgent decisions. The problem arises when this automatic thinking spills over into areas such as personal growth or health, where adhering to old patterns can leave us stuck and unfulfilled.

Let me tell you about my friend Emily. She decided it was time to get in shape a few years ago. Like many people, she went all in, signing up for a gym membership and committing to hit the treadmill five days a week. At first, she was excited. That excitement, however, quickly faded. Within a couple of weeks, the routine felt like a grind. She started skipping workouts. By the end of the month, she had not stepped foot inside the gym, although her membership fees kept coming out of her account.

Frustrated and defeated, Emily said, "Maybe I am just not cut out for this." She was ready to throw in the towel altogether.

I encouraged her to call her approach to fitness "New Choice." Instead of pushing herself to stick with a plan that clearly was not working, I suggested she try something completely different, even if it felt a little unconventional.

The next day, Emily swapped her treadmill session for a dance class. It was way out of her comfort zone, primarily since she had never danced before. By the end of the class, she was laughing and sweating, and for the first time, exercise did not feel like a chore. It felt like fun.

Over the next few weeks, Emily began exploring other "New Choices." She went hiking, tried yoga, and even gave kickboxing a shot. Not everything worked. Kickboxing was a one-and-done, but she discovered activities that she genuinely enjoyed. Exercise became something she looked forward to, not dreaded. By allowing herself to pivot, Emily found a way to prioritize her health while reconnecting with joy and curiosity.

Her story proves that "New Choice" is not just for the big, life-changing decisions. Sometimes, it is about trying a fresh approach to the same goal. When Emily let go of her all-or-nothing mindset, she developed a sustainable approach to caring for herself without forcing it.

The takeaway here is simple: "New Choice" is about recognizing where you are stuck and giving yourself the freedom to try something new, even if it feels uncomfortable or unconventional at first. Whether it is your workout routine, how you approach relationships, or how you spend your weekends, calling "New Choice" can help you break out of old habits and discover new possibilities you never imagined.

Psychologist Adam Grant's research in *Think Again* expands on this same principle. His studies on rethinking reveal that our strongest leaders, and happiest individuals, aren't those who cling to their original beliefs, but those willing to update them when new evidence emerges. Grant calls this the power of "cognitive flexibility" - the ability to pivot without losing your identity. The "New Choice" mindset operates in exactly that space. It teaches your brain to associate change with growth, not threat; curiosity, not fear. Each time you make a new choice, you strengthen neural pathways linked to learning and adaptability.

The act of rethinking, whether in leadership, relationships, or daily habits, is not about admitting you were wrong; it's about proving you're still learning. That's what "New Choice" trains you to do: see pivoting as progress and movement as mastery.

The Science of Choice

Our brains operate much like GPS systems. When faced with a decision, they instinctively chart the easiest and most familiar route, the one with the least resistance. This process is efficient, saving mental energy. Still, it also keeps us stuck in routines that may no longer serve us. Calling "New Choice" is the mental equivalent of pressing the recalibrate button on your GPS. Stepping off the familiar path activates parts of the brain wired for discovery, unlocking ideas and outcomes that routine thinking would never surface.

Recalibrating your thoughts can feel deeply uncomfortable. The brain resists change, clinging to safety and predictability even when both come at the cost of growth. During a recent "New Choice" exercise with a group of executives, I noticed their hesitation as they struggled to step outside their comfort zones. Their resistance highlighted the familiar pull of default patterns; those deeply ingrained habits we all rely on. Neuroscience helps explain this phenomenon.

Survival instincts pull us toward the familiar, reinforcing habits that feel safe even when they keep us stuck. However, the exact mechanisms that shield us from risk can also prevent us from growing.

By learning to recalibrate and embrace the discomfort of change, we can overcome these instincts and start exploring new possibilities.

Why We Stick to Defaults

Our brains naturally favor the path of least resistance for several reasons. First, we tend to gravitate toward the familiar because familiar choices feel safe. They reduce mental stress and provide a comforting sense of control. Habits often stay in place long after they've outlived their usefulness simply because they *feel* familiar, and familiarity feels safe.

Try this. In one of Dr. Sivasailam "Thiagi" Thiagarajan's well-known facilitation exercises, participants are asked to say the days of the week in order. Easy enough. Then they're asked to do it again, but this time, in alphabetical order. Suddenly, what seemed effortless becomes awkward. There's hesitation, laughter, and even mild frustration.

This simple activity reveals how strongly our brains cling to existing mental patterns. We don't question the default order because it's ingrained through repetition. When we're asked to rearrange what we know, our brains resist, searching for a new map that doesn't yet exist. That micro-moment of confusion mirrors what happens every time we face change. Even small shifts can feel disorienting because the mind equates different with difficult. That brief discomfort is a window into our default wiring. The same mental resistance that makes it hard to alphabetize the days of the week also shows up in bigger life decisions.

Second, we seek validation. Our minds crave evidence that confirms we're on the right track. Without realizing it, we filter out information that challenges our beliefs and cling to what feels right instead. Psychologists call this confirmation bias, and it acts like a comfort blanket for the brain. The craving for certainty clouds judgment, making unfamiliar options feel dangerous, even when they offer something better.

Lastly, we fear loss. Change inherently feels risky. Neuroscience shows that humans are wired to overestimate potential losses and undervalue potential gains. Known as loss aversion, this bias keeps us anchored to the status quo, holding tightly to what we know, even when the alternative could be better.

Such tendencies, while rooted in survival, are the same patterns that often prevent us from evolving and embracing new opportunities. The goal isn't to eliminate these instincts but to become aware of them. Once we recognize the defaults running the show, we can consciously interrupt them with a new choice, a moment of mindful disruption that reintroduces curiosity where comfort once ruled.

So, the next time you find yourself stuck in an old pattern, imagine you're reciting the days of the week in alphabetical order. It might feel awkward at first, but that's the sound of your brain waking up to possibility.

How "New Choice" Breaks the Cycle

The "New Choice" framework offers a practical approach to retraining your brain. Quick, low-stakes decisions interrupt the brain's usual resistance and create space for new neural pathways to form. Each time you engage in this practice, you build confidence by taking action, even when uncertainty lingers in the background. Instead of viewing failure as a dead end, you see it as valuable feedback, allowing you to pivot and move forward rather than remaining stuck. Over time, you strengthen your ability to adapt, turning flexibility into a skill you can rely on in every area of life.

When you embrace "New Choice," you break free from the default patterns that hold you back and unlock your potential for creative possibilities. Adaptability is not simply a fixed trait; it is a muscle that grows stronger each time you call "New Choice."

The Three Elements of Effective Pivots

Through years of teaching this method, I have identified three key elements that distinguish successful pivots from unsuccessful ones. The first is awareness. This involves recognizing your default patterns and becoming more conscious of the moments when a decision needs to be made. Emotional triggers shape how you respond to change. Spotting them early helps you pause, pivot, and choose more intentionally when pressure hits.

The second element is permission. Permitting yourself to change is essential, especially when you feel tethered to past choices or outcomes. It means letting go of the idea that every decision must be perfect and instead embracing imperfection as part of the process. Releasing this attachment creates the freedom to try something new.

Finally, there is practice. Successful pivots often start with bold choices, even small ones, that allow you to build your decision-making muscles over time. Creating a supportive environment through trusted relationships or systems that encourage experimentation helps reinforce this practice. With repetition, these elements become second nature, making it easier to pivot with confidence and clarity.

Your First New Choice

Following the initial demonstration, a remarkable event occurred during the training session. The executives began to apply the concept to real challenges they were facing. One product manager decided to call "New Choice" on a launch strategy that had not been working, exploring a completely new approach. A team leader reimagined a difficult conversation with a direct report, finding a way to navigate it with greater clarity and empathy. Meanwhile, a director uncovered a creative solution to a budget constraint that no one had considered before.

The energy in the room became electric. People who had been skeptical only hours earlier were now eagerly sharing how to use this framework professionally and personally. Clearly, "New Choice" was more than a game; it was a tool for unlocking potential and embracing new possibilities.

Making It Real

The power of "New Choice" does not come from the game itself, but from how it rewires our approach to decision-making. To start applying it in your own life, begin by noticing your defaults. Spend a week tracking your daily decisions and pay attention to the patterns that emerge. Are there automatic responses or routines that you rely on without thinking? Question those defaults and consider whether they still serve you or if they are simply habits born from familiarity.

Next, practice small pivots. You do not have to overhaul your life overnight. Start with something simple, like taking a different route to work or changing one element of your daily routine. Even small changes, like responding differently to a typical situation, can create ripple effects that lead to new opportunities and perspectives.

As you continue, work on building your "New Choice" muscles. Start with low-stakes decisions to develop confidence and adaptability. Over time, gradually increase the complexity of the choices you experiment with. Celebrate your successful pivots, no matter how small they seem, because each represents progress in shifting your mindset and embracing flexibility.

With consistent practice, calling "New Choice" will become second nature. Over time, utilizing the "New Choice" mindset shifts from technique to instinct, fueling your life with creativity, courage, and possibility.

Encore: Every Choice Is a New Beginning

Every moment holds the possibility of a new beginning. "New Choice" is more than a clever improv tool or a creative warm-up because it disrupts decision-making. A reminder that no matter how stuck you feel, you're always one pivot away from momentum.

You've now seen how fast, low-stakes shifts in thinking can rewire the brain, interrupt default patterns, and strengthen your ability to adapt in real time. The game works because it demands presence, silences perfectionism, and rewards boldness over polish. Each pivot is practice. Each change trains your brain to expect options instead of obstacles.

When paired with the "Yes, And" mindset, your choices stop competing with your reality and start building on it. You begin to say, "This is what I have… and here's what I can do next."

The power lies in noticing your patterns, permitting yourself to choose again, and practicing until that flexibility becomes second nature. No big declaration required. Just a quiet, steady rhythm of choosing forward instead of freezing in place.

If one choice gets you stuck, another can get you out. Every "New Choice" begins with a single word: Yes.

Scene Work:

Take the stage and move from theory to practice with these quick drills to help you catch your defaults, pivot in the moment, and train your brain for change.

- Notice Your Default Patterns: Track one recurring decision you make automatically for three days. Write down what triggered it, what you chose, and how it felt afterward.

- Practice the "New Choice" Game: Choose one small daily decision and deliberately make a different choice tomorrow. Start simple: take a different route, order something new, or change your morning routine.

- Start a Decision Journal: For one week, record one significant choice you made each day, noting your reasoning and the outcome. Look for patterns in your decision-making style.

Side Coaching:

Before making more choices, pause and check in. The following prompts will help you be honest about what's on autopilot and what needs to change.

- What default patterns do you notice most in your decision-making?

- Where do you most wish you could call "New Choice"?

- What's the smallest pivot you could make today that might create the most significant shift?

Script Revision:

Every rehearsal ends with a new line to carry forward. Rewrite your script let it guide your next decision:

"I can choose differently at any moment. Every choice is a chance to grow."

Chapter 2:
Choosing The Improvised Path

How Theater Games Became Survival Skills

"Life is an improvisation. You have no idea what's going to happen next and you are mostly just making things up as you go along." — Stephen Colbert

Before I discuss the history of improvisation and its impact on social work and entertainment, I need to explain what improv is NOT. It is not stand-up comedy, though many associate it with the same skill set. Misunderstanding the difference can be problematic when explaining the value of improv in emotional intelligence and business.

Understanding Improvisation (Improv) Versus Stand-Up Comedy

One of my biggest challenges as the owner of an improv comedy training center and theatre (Carolina Improv Company) has been explaining exactly what improv is and what it is not. The art form is often confused with stand-up comedy. While the two share similarities, improv focuses on ensemble (team) performance, while stand-up is a solo (silo) act. The confusion grew with the rise of The Improv Comedy Clubs.

The Improv Comedy Club chain, founded by Budd Friedman in New York City in 1963, has a rich history. Initially conceived as a coffee house for Broadway performers to gather and engage in spontaneous performances after their shows, it quickly transformed into America's first dedicated stand-up comedy venue. The term "improv" originally referred to the unrehearsed nature of these performances, but over time, the focus shifted towards comedians using the stage to test new material. The Improv hosted legendary comedians like Richard Pryor, George Carlin, and Robin Williams, who honed their craft on its stage. The club's atmosphere fostered creativity and collaboration, making it a vital launching pad for many comedy careers.

By the late 1970s, The Improv expanded beyond New York City, opening a second location in Los Angeles in 1974. This expansion continued throughout the 1980s and 1990s, opening clubs in various cities across the United States. I was even part of that expansion in the late 1980s when I joined the original staff of the Chicago location as a cocktail waitress and met many famous comedians. As an aspiring actress, I was inspired to be part of the atmosphere. The Improv also gained national recognition through the television series "An Evening at the Improv," which aired from 1982 to 1996 and showcased performances from many emerging comedians.

The club's evolution paralleled the growth of The Second City in Chicago, where comedy was improvised and not scripted like stand-up comedy. The Improv Comedy Clubs still exist in multiple cities, perpetuating the confusion between improv and stand-up. I often find myself explaining the differences to strangers who see me wearing my branded "Carolina Improv" shirt and ask which famous comedians are currently performing at my club. The general public's misunderstanding extends beyond the public when I'm promoting improv as a tool for organizational development. When C-Suite executives hear "improv," they fear our training will put them (and their teams) in vulnerable, uncomfortable situations on stage, expecting them to be funny. My goal with this book is to debunk that perception while showing how improv principles fuel The New Choice Effect, a practical framework for resilience, creativity, and emotional intelligence. I have also coined this "Improvised Intelligence.™"

": My goal with this book is to debunk that perception while showing how improv principles fuel The New Choice Effect, a practical framework for resilience, creativity, and emotional intelligence. I have also coined this "Improvised Intelligence."™

To help potential clients understand the difference between improv and stand-up comedy, I typically ask them if they've seen or heard of the TV show "Whose Line Is It Anyway," which was first popularized in the UK and later in the US with Drew Carey as the host. In that show, performers improvise as a team, relying on audience suggestions and pre-determined "games," which I'll share later in this book. Nothing is scripted; the players depend on improvisational theatre's tenets (rules). Many are surprised to learn that improv has a framework. Once you master these guidelines, creating and responding in the moment appear seamless and fluid.

During my early years of improv, I didn't know anything about emotional intelligence, the power of improv for business applications, or the neuroscience involved. Still, I knew that the improv games I was learning were transformative for my mindset and career trajectory. My attitude and drive had completely changed during my college years. I grew up with a negative mother who projected her lack of accomplishments on me while putting me down for my dreams. Even with my more positive father, I was raised to believe I was limited to the expectations of getting married and having children. With every failure and success I experienced in improv exercises, I continued to build self and social awareness and became more emotionally intelligent without realizing it. What I didn't realize at the time was that these improv practices were shaping the foundation of what I now call The New Choice Effect. Before we dive deeper into that framework, let's explore the roots and history of improv.

The History of Improv: Commedia dell'arte

Improvisation has been part of theatrical traditions for centuries, evolving through a rich history of spontaneous and unscripted performances dating back to 1570. It played a crucial role in Commedia dell'arte, an Italian theater form that gained popularity throughout Europe. Commedia dell'arte was characterized by its use of masked stock characters, physical comedy, and a structured yet improvised performance style. These stock characters, often clichéd figures,

represented specific stereotypes or types, making them instantly recognizable to audiences. Examples include the "damsel in distress," the "mad scientist," and the "noble hero."

The renown of Commedia dell'arte performances was chiefly attributed to the art of improvisation. This improvisational element brought a distinctive allure to the theatrical experience, especially within the broader framework of Renaissance culture and its rhetorical heritage, which heavily relied on imitation and memory. In this context, imitation and memory were not merely viewed as the replication and repetition of skills but rather as creative arts themselves, contributing to the process of invention during a time when literacy was not widespread. This art form also laid the foundation for Vaudeville entertainment and slapstick (physical) comedy in the late 19th century.

20th Century Improv: Neva Boyd & Viola Spolin

One significant milestone in the development of improv is often associated with the work of Viola Spolin, the "mother of improv," who started her groundbreaking work in the 1920s in Chicago. Spolin, an American educator and theater artist, pioneered the development of improvisational techniques. She began experimenting with theater games and exercises to teach drama and enhance creativity. Her work paved the way for what would later become known as improvisational theatre. The techniques she developed were further popularized by her son, Paul Sills, and his involvement in the Compass Players and later The Second City improvisational comedy troupe.

Spolin's groundbreaking book, "Improvisation for the Theater," published in 1963, significantly impacted American theater, television, and film, providing new tools and techniques for actors, directors, and writers. Interestingly, it took her about 40 years to publish this book. Her transformative journey began at age 18 in 1924 when she became a Chicago settlement house (Hull House) worker. Then and there, she met Neva Boyd, an American sociologist at Hull House in Chicago, who trained, mentored, and inspired her.

Understanding Boyd's impact before further delving into Spolin's effect on the world of improv is essential. Despite my three decades of experience in the improv realm, the intricacies of how Spolin acquired her insights into the application of improv remained elusive. What proved even more significant was the profound influence of Neva Boyd on Spolin's work. My contemplation on whether to investigate this aspect initially slowed down the writing of this book. However, my decision to explore it has brought newfound clarity. Understanding the application of improv in social work during the early 1920s has deepened my perspective, providing a clearer understanding of improv as a modality for enhancing emotional intelligence, human connection, and relationship management.

Boyd, considered an education trailblazer, established the Recreational Training School, giving training opportunities to young social workers. She crafted a unique one-year educational program that taught educators the importance of encouraging meaningful play for children and adults, especially immigrants. This program was a vibrant tapestry of experiences, weaving together group games, gymnastics, dancing, dramatic arts, play theory, and insightful discussions on social problems.

She emphasized the cognitive significance of group play theory, considering play as a universal behavior transcending cultural and historical boundaries. Boyd believed in the inherent social values of human play and viewed it as a biological necessity crucial for human development rather than merely a voluntary activity. Utilizing games, later evolving into improv games, and play as tools in her social work, she aimed to impart essential life skills such as language, problem-solving, self-confidence, and socialization. Boyd regarded games as organized accumulations of play behavior, mainly rooted in the thalamic region of the nervous system, closely linked to the outside world, thus providing every participant access to the stimulation of this dynamic process.

Moving into the 1940s, Boyd's methods extended their reach to every U.S. military hospital established by the Red Cross. Here, wounded veterans engaged in playful games crafted by Boyd, preparing them for the transition back to their lives. Additionally, she realized that play activities could be applied to effectively communicate with hard-to-reach individuals, leading her to introduce group play's educational and therapeutic values in specialized settings in hospitals throughout Illinois.

Boyd's enduring impact extends into the realm of "medical improv," a contemporary training modality. Actively engaged in teaching health practitioners, I guide them to enhance empathy with patients through improv games, tapping into their social skills. This demonstrates the continued relevance of Boyd's pioneering work in various settings, fostering well-being and social harmony, from settlement houses to military hospitals.

Neva Boyd's educational program, incorporating improv in social group work, laid the foundation for future drama education, entertainment, and healthcare development. The growth of improv, a byproduct of turbulent times, can be attributed, in my opinion, to these two powerful women who pioneered change, contributing to the betterment of the world through humanization. Boyd's visionary approach resonates in diverse fields, shaping the trajectory of drama education and its applications in entertainment and healthcare.

Boyd's pioneering use of improv as a tool for nurturing social skills grounded in empathy left an enduring impact on Viola Spolin. Inspired by Boyd's approach, Spolin embarked on a mission to help her students recognize the universal benefits of dramatic play. This inclusive vision encompassed people with disabilities, the illiterate, and those living in extreme poverty. The result was the development of hundreds of theatre games, rooted in Boyd's theories and methods, during the 1930s and 1940s.

In 1945, Boyd released the "Handbook of Games," later reprinted as the "Handbook of Recreational Games," which featured a collection of folk dances and social activities from various cultures, previously unpublished. This comprehensive guide quickly became a valuable resource for educators, parents, and recreation and playground management professionals. While there is no definite confirmation, it is plausible that Boyd's book was a reference for Spolin's Theatre Games, as several games from Boyd's compilation are found within Spolin's work.

Spolin's innovative techniques were designed to dismantle barriers, foster spontaneity, and instill a profound sense of play. She firmly believed that engaging in creative games and activities enabled individuals to unlock their inner creativity and cultivate essential skills like communication, collaboration, and problem-solving. Spolin's reinterpretation of Boyd's ideas influenced her immediate theatre students and shaped the practices of 1960s companies like the Open Theater, the Living Theatre, and The Second City. Improvisation became the heartbeat of these avant-garde ensembles, a shared language for spontaneous, collective creation.

The Growth of Improv: Players Workshop, The Second City, and Saturday Night Live

Inspired by his mother Viola Spolin and her innovative theater games, Paul Sills embarked on a journey to develop and popularize improvisational theater with her invaluable assistance. In the mid-1950s, he co-founded the Playwrights Theatre Club with fellow students from the University of Chicago's dramatics club, due to the absence of a formal drama department. Sills initiated workshops based on his mother's theater games, aiming to assemble an ensemble for Compass Players, a revue-style theater venture.

Amidst the evolving theatrical landscape, another pioneering figure, Josephine ("Jo") Raciti-Forsberg, emerged as a transformative presence alongside Viola Spolin, Paul Sills, and Playwrights Producer David Shepherd. Together, they introduced fundamental elements like "The Game" and "The Rules" of improvisation, notably the early foundation of the "Yes, And" principle, which I've previously mentioned in this book. Their collaboration laid the groundwork for what would later become the cornerstone of modern improvisational theater.

The evolution continued as Compass Players transitioned into The Second City Theatre in 1959, spearheaded by Bernie Sahlins, Howard Alk, and others. The transition marked a turning point in the global rise of improvisational theater and opened the door to a new era of sharp, satirical storytelling, an evolution I'll unpack as we move through this chapter.

Spolin's influence reverberated within The Second City as she conducted workshops, sparking creativity among cast members. Initially an understudy, Forsberg immersed herself in improvisational classes under Spolin's guidance. Forsberg's profound understanding of Spolin's techniques earned her the role of Spolin's assistant teacher, cementing her pivotal role in shaping The Second City's trajectory.

As Spolin departed Chicago for Los Angeles in the mid-1960s, Forsberg assumed leadership of her workshops at The Second City. She produced children's shows and eventually established an official school of improvisation, Players Workshop of The Second City, in 1971. This transformative venture, blending Spolin's teachings with Forsberg's vision, became the epicenter of improvisational theater education.

The relationship between Players Workshop and The Second City Training Center became symbiotic. Aspiring performers, including myself, often began their journey at Players Workshop, with completion guaranteeing entry into The Second City Training Center without the required audition others endured. Both institutions experienced significant growth, with Players Workshop reaching over 500 students in 1989.

Jo's legacy, intertwined with Viola Spolin's teachings, continues to reverberate in the realm of improvisational theater, leaving an indelible mark on the art form and the communities it

touches. Beyond The Second City, she nurtured talents like David Mamet, Bill Murray, Harold Ramis, Betty Thomas, Shelley Long, and George Wendt, while impacting countless others, including this author from 1987 to 1992. Her unwavering dedication to her students' growth, coupled with her deep exploration of psychological principles, positioned her as a teacher, mentor, and friend. Jo became my surrogate mother at a volatile time in my life when I needed direction, guidance, and unconditional love. Her passion and dedication inspired me to create and open my own improv training center nearly three decades after taking my first improv class.

The Second City Training Center continues to flourish, attracting actors from around the globe, each aspiring to be the next Tina Fey, Amy Poehler, Rachel Dratch, Stephen Colbert, Steve Carrell, or Jim Belushi. The training ground buzzes with the energy of hopefuls, vying to become celebrities. Navigating through this creative landscape in my early 20s, I initially harbored dreams of being discovered on The Second City mainstage, hoping to catch the eye of Lorne Michaels, producer of the TV show Saturday Night Live.

Michaels regularly flew from New York City to Chicago to scout new talent. However, reality reshaped my path, guiding me toward entertainment's operations and production side. While I wasn't destined to be an accountant, as originally planned, I had enough mathematical acumen to know that the probability of "being discovered" was low, and I was okay with that. Improv classes helped me uncover talents that would later serve me and others in more meaningfully ways.

Encore: From Performance To Mindset

Improvisation didn't start on a comedy stage, and it's not just about being funny. Long before it landed on stage, improv served as a lifeline for expression, survival, and human connection, from the marketplaces of Renaissance Italy to the classrooms of early social workers in Chicago. The history of improv is filled with bold women, smart rebellion, and a relentless belief in what's possible when people play with purpose.

For decades, pioneers like Neva Boyd, Viola Spolin, and Jo Forsberg used improvisation to teach empathy, restore confidence, and build community. Their work laid the foundation for entertainment empires like Second City and Saturday Night Live, but the deeper magic was always emotional intelligence, not punchlines.

Today, improv continues to evolve, not as a performance gimmick, but as a real-life training ground for flexibility, curiosity, and growth. At its core, it teaches one truth: you don't need to know what's next. You just need to stay present and respond with courage.

Skip the script and be willing to show up and say "Yes, And."

Chapter 3:
Choosing To Rewire Your Brain

The Neuroscience of Getting Unstuck and Making Bolder Moves

"Your brain is wired for survival, not for clarity, but the more you train it, the faster you can pivot from reaction to response." — Anonymous

Daily, you make approximately 35,000 decisions, from what to wear to which strategic direction will define your company's future. Yet despite this constant practice, decision-making remains one of the most challenging aspects of leadership and life. The problem isn't that we lack intelligence, experience, or good intentions. The problem is that our brains, environments, and even our success patterns can become the obstacles that prevent us from choosing boldly and moving forward decisively.

After working with leaders and teams across countless industries, I've identified the core barriers that transform what should be straightforward choices into exhausting internal battles:

1. Psychological Barriers

The internal obstacles we create are often the most formidable. Fear of failure consistently ranks as the primary factor that causes capable leaders and team members to hesitate when decisive action is needed. When combined with perfectionism, this fear creates a cycle of analysis paralysis. In this state, individuals become so focused on identifying the perfect solution that they exhaust their mental resources without progressing. Self-doubt compounds these challenges by undermining confidence in judgment, creating uncertainty even when the path seems clear.

Perhaps most significantly, negative past experiences cast long shadows over present decisions, causing individuals to perceive current choices as more complex or risky than they are. These psychological patterns distort our view of what's possible and often keep us from choosing, not because we lack options, but because we fear getting it wrong.

2. Environmental Challenges

External pressures compound internal struggles. With thousands of daily decisions competing for mental bandwidth, decision fatigue becomes inevitable, leaving us mentally depleted when important choices arise. The paradox of choice creates additional complexity, while options seem beneficial, too many alternatives can overwhelm our cognitive capacity and lead to decision paralysis. Information overload presents a particularly modern challenge: we're simultaneously drowning in data while lacking the specific insights needed to move forward confidently. This creates a frustrating cycle of too much information and ambiguity.

3. Cognitive Biases

Our brains contain built-in shortcuts that can sabotage even our best intentions. Status quo bias keeps us anchored to familiar approaches, even when we recognize the need for change.

Anchoring bias causes us to fixate on the first piece of information we encounter, making it challenging to consider superior alternatives that emerge later. Confirmation bias leads us to seek information supporting our beliefs while dismissing contradictory evidence. Pressure amplifies these cognitive distortions, pushing us toward mental shortcuts that feel efficient but often lead to suboptimal outcomes.

4. Fresh Approach to Decision-Making

Recognizing these barriers represents the first step toward transformation. Moving beyond them requires a different approach entirely. Improvisation offers a powerful solution, extending beyond its theatrical origins to become a practical framework for decision-making excellence.

Rather than fighting against uncertainty, improvisation teaches us to work with ambiguity as a creative force. Rather than seeking perfect information, improvisation shows us how to make confident choices with what we have. By embracing principles like "New Choice" and "Yes, And," we can transform decision-making from an exhausting internal battle into an energizing process of discovery and growth.

How Improvisation Unlocks Better Decisions

Improvisation often conjures images of quick-witted performers navigating unscripted moments, yet the principles extend far beyond the stage. The concepts of "New Choice" and "Yes, And" offer transformative potential in every area of personal life, helping you break out of limiting patterns, embrace challenges, and build resilience. Life's complexities, from relationships and health to career and purpose, can benefit from these tools' creativity, adaptability, and intentionality.

"New Choice" centers on recognizing when you are stuck in a default pattern and actively choosing a different path. You might abandon ineffective study habits or self-limiting beliefs in education and learning to try a new approach that sparks curiosity. For your career, making a new choice could be the push to leave an unfulfilling job and explore a role that aligns with your passions and skills. While often uncomfortable, these shifts rewire your brain to prioritize growth and innovation over the safety of the familiar.

"Yes, And" takes the concept further by encouraging you to acknowledge your current reality and build on what exists. Rather than avoiding challenges or pretending everything is perfect, the principle helps you lean into the present moment and ask, "What can I add to the situation?" In financial wellbeing, "Yes, And" might mean acknowledging current financial struggles while brainstorming creative ways to save, invest, or increase income. Family dynamics can transform when you accept past conflicts while focusing on actions that foster stronger connections moving forward.

Every area of life can benefit from these principles. Home and environment decisions might involve reevaluating how you use your space to ensure comfort and productivity support. "Yes, And" could encourage you to make the most of what you already have while envisioning how to create an ideal environment. Love and relationships flourish when "New Choice" empowers you to recognize unhelpful patterns and take intentional steps to strengthen your bond. "Yes, And" encourages deeper connection by affirming your partner's strengths while working collaboratively toward shared goals.

Community connections can deepen when "New Choice" leads you to prioritize meaningful relationships over surface-level interactions. "Yes, And" adds a layer of openness, allowing you to engage fully with those around you and say yes to opportunities to give back or connect on a deeper level. Personal growth and identity development accelerate when these tools encourage you to embrace new hobbies, self-discovery practices, or bold changes, helping you grow into your best self.

Health and wellness journeys transform through these principles. "New Choice" helps break free from unsustainable habits, like skipping workouts or eating poorly, while "Yes, And" encourages you to find joy in small, positive changes. Try a new exercise routine or build healthier meals around your favorite foods.

Spiritual connection can evolve when "New Choice" allows you to rethink rigid beliefs or practices that no longer resonate with you, while "Yes, And" fosters openness, encouraging the integration of spirituality into your daily life in a meaningful and personal way.

Embracing "New Choice" and "Yes, And" in every facet of life allows you to move beyond default reactions and create a mindset of curiosity and adaptability. Rather than just solving immediate problems, these tools create a foundation for long-term growth and transformation. The chapters ahead will dive into each area, showing how to apply these principles in practical, actionable ways to reshape your life with creativity, confidence, and purpose. Whether navigating family relationships, redefining your career, or pursuing personal growth, these tools give you the power to move forward with intention and possibility.

The Neuroscience of Improvisation

Improvisation creates profound changes in brain activity, fostering creativity and adaptability through measurable neural shifts. Neuroscientists Charles Limb and Allen Braun made a groundbreaking discovery when studying musicians improvising inside fMRI machines. The dorsolateral prefrontal cortex part of the brain, responsible for self-criticism and analytical judgment, essentially shuts down during improvisation. Simultaneously, the brain's creative regions activate with remarkable intensity.

Limb and Braun identified this phenomenon as "weak connectivity in the executive control network," which allows the brain to enter a flow state where creativity emerges naturally without the interference of self-doubt. Even more remarkably, researcher Martin Norgaard found that visualizing improvisation produces similar patterns of creative neural activation. The brain responds to imagined improvisation nearly as powerfully as the experience.

The "Yes, And" principle leverages this neurological foundation by creating the psychological safety necessary for exploration and innovation. "Yes, And" trains the brain to override automatic rejection responses and remain receptive to new possibilities. Rather than simply representing a positive mindset, "Yes, And" triggers measurable neurological changes that enable us to approach challenges with curiosity instead of defensiveness. Regular practice strengthens these neural pathways, making creative problem-solving and bold decision-making more accessible over time.

Breaking Default Patterns

The brain operates as an efficiency-focused system, relying on familiar patterns to conserve energy. The basal ganglia in the forebrain, which govern habits and routines, play a central role in automating repetitive behaviors. While these patterns serve us well for routine tasks, they can limit creativity and adaptability when innovation is required.

The "New Choice" framework disrupts these habitual responses by encouraging intentional action. Choosing to approach a situation differently, whether through a fresh problem-solving method, a new interaction style, or an unconventional approach, interrupts the brain's default wiring. Conscious decision-making engages the prefrontal cortex, the region responsible for deliberate thinking and strategic planning.

Consider a workplace conflict where the natural tendency might be avoidance. Choosing instead to address the situation constructively while applying a "Yes, And" mindset allows you to acknowledge the other person's perspective and build upon it. Deliberate choices like these create opportunities for solutions that might otherwise remain hidden. The brain begins to rewire itself, favoring adaptability over avoidance.

Improvisation demonstrates how stepping outside habitual responses activates different neural pathways. An improviser replaces predictable "No" or "Yes, but" reactions with "Yes, And," fostering creativity and flexibility. Regular practice makes the brain increasingly open to change and better equipped to navigate challenges while unlocking new possibilities.

Creating New Neural Pathways

Neuroplasticity, the brain's ability to adapt and rewire, provides the foundation for lasting transformation. Each new choice creates a "trail" in your brain that strengthens with repetition, eventually forming a new pathway. Picture forging a path through dense forest: the more you walk, the clearer and easier it becomes to navigate. Default patterns in the brain resemble well-worn trails, familiar and automatic. Improvisation encourages the creation of entirely new routes.

The "Yes, And" principle enhances neuroplasticity by promoting openness to unexpected opportunities and seamlessly integrating new ideas. Rather than resisting change, you learn to build upon what's presented, fostering flexibility and adaptability. Over time, this rewiring shifts your entire mindset, helping you approach challenges and opportunities with curiosity and confidence.

Sara Lazar's landmark study at Harvard University demonstrates how consistent mental practices physically alter brain structure. Her team found that regular meditation increases thickness in the prefrontal cortex, which governs decision-making and attention, and the insula, which manages emotional awareness. These findings reveal the biological foundation for our capacity to adapt and grow.

Similarly, practicing improvisation strengthens neural pathways associated with cognitive flexibility and emotional intelligence, creating a more responsive and resilient brain. Every attempt to try something new pushes your brain to form fresh neural connections. Daniel Goleman's work on emotional intelligence shows that EQ can be developed throughout our lives. Improv accelerates this development by creating safe spaces to practice the very skills Goleman identifies: recognizing emotions in yourself and others, managing your responses, and navigating relationships with greater awareness. Improvisational techniques prove particularly effective because they train the brain to embrace the unfamiliar while breaking old patterns and encouraging resilience.

Neuroplasticity confirms that change remains possible at any stage of life. Whether learning a new skill, adopting a different perspective, or taking bold steps forward, each effort to embrace novelty strengthens your brain's capacity for growth and transformation.

Cognitive Benefits: Expanding Mental Flexibility

Improvisation transforms how your brain processes information and generates solutions. Research by Hainselin, Aubry, and Bourdin (2018) demonstrated this effect in a study titled *"Improving Teenagers' Divergent Thinking With Improvisational Theater."* Middle school students who participated in an 11-week improvisation program showed significant improvements in originality and cognitive flexibility compared to peers engaged in traditional activities such as sports. Even brief exposure to improvisation can strengthen your ability to approach challenges with innovative solutions and adaptive thinking.

Research on Decision-Making

Improvisation extends beyond creativity to encompass rapid, confident decision-making. During improvisation, the analytical mind that typically leads to overthinking and paralysis becomes quieter, allowing you to bypass hesitation under pressure. Improvisers develop the ability to trust their instincts and embrace uncertainty, resulting in faster and more effective decision-making.

Whether determining the next line in a comedy scene or the next strategic move in a boardroom, improv trains the brain to prioritize action over analysis. Leaders and professionals who develop this skill can tackle crises, adapt to shifting circumstances, and make thoughtful decisions in real time while maintaining clarity and confidence.

Unlocking Better Choices

The mental health benefits of improvisation directly translate to enhanced decision-making capabilities. Increased confidence and improved emotional regulation reduce the stress associated with high-pressure choices, while cultivated calmness fosters clear and deliberate action.

Decision-making represents a crucial intersection between improvisation and neuroscience. Research shows that the brain naturally gravitates toward habitual choices, even when those choices no longer serve us well. The brain's preference for predictability makes familiar options feel safer than new alternatives, creating cognitive patterns that reinforce predictable behavior and keep us trapped in routines that may no longer align with our goals.

The New Choice Effect provides a powerful method for breaking this cycle. By intentionally making different decisions, you override the brain's default settings and create opportunities for better outcomes. Improvisation amplifies this process in real time, particularly when combined with the "Yes, And" principle. Using "Yes, And" during brainstorming sessions can generate innovative solutions that might never emerge if new ideas were immediately dismissed or resisted.

Practicing improvisation develops the ability to pause, reflect, and consider alternatives that might otherwise go unexplored. Research demonstrates that this approach enhances problem-solving, teamwork, and leadership skills across various contexts.

While traditional models once emphasized the amygdala as the brain's "fear center," newer research has shown that emotions are distributed throughout the brain, influencing decision-making in complex, integrated ways. When faced with uncertainty, emotional responses can override rational thought, triggering instinctive reactions such as fight-or-flight. Improvisation counteracts this effect by introducing curiosity and playfulness, which calm reactive neural patterns and reengage the brain's higher-order thinking systems.

This is why "Yes, And" feels empowering; it transforms fear into possibility. By doing so, improvisation creates mental space where intentional, creative decisions can flourish.

Why We Get Stuck in Patterns

Feeling stuck often stems from the brain's natural tendency to prioritize familiarity. Habits, routines, and limiting beliefs become deeply ingrained through repetition, forming mental ruts that prove difficult to escape. Fear of failure or judgment compounds this challenge by activating the brain's threat response, reinforcing cycles of avoidance and preventing exploration of new possibilities.

The New Choice Effect, combined with the practice of "Yes, And" effectively disrupts these patterns. Reframing fear as an opportunity for growth weakens the grip of old habits and beliefs. Making small, intentional choices to act differently creates momentum and opens doors to transformation. Approaching challenges with "Yes, And" turns obstacles into opportunities, fostering creativity and resilience instead of stagnation.

Consider someone who struggles with public speaking and defaults to avoidance. Despite discomfort, choosing to accept a small speaking opportunity disrupts that pattern. Pairing this choice with "Yes, And" by affirming existing strengths while embracing feedback encourages progress and builds confidence over time. Small, consistent actions eventually become second nature, diminishing the power of fear.

The science of improvisation explains why this approach works so effectively. Repeated behaviors reinforce habits and beliefs, making them automatic and resistant to change. Improvisation trains the brain to reframe uncertainty as a challenge rather than a threat. By stepping outside comfort zones and embracing the unknown, individuals weaken the hold of old patterns while building the adaptability needed to thrive in new situations.

Science Meets the New Choice Framework

Improvisation's power lies in combining scientific understanding with practical transformation. Understanding how the brain defaults to habits, responds to fear, and forms new pathways enables you to use principles like "Yes, And" and "New Choice" to rewire thought patterns

deliberately. Improvisation extends beyond solving immediate problems to foster a mindset that thrives on adaptability and creativity.

Each time you choose "Yes, And" instead of resistance, or make a new choice instead of repeating old behaviors, you strengthen the brain's capacity to embrace change. Small, intentional decisions help with immediate challenges while building a foundation for resilience, resourcefulness, and alignment with your fullest potential.

Improvisation blends creativity with structure, spontaneity with intentionality. Research confirms that disrupting default patterns, creating new neural pathways, and reframing decision-making can unlock hidden potential. Change becomes not just possible but essential for personal growth.

Your brain is designed to evolve when you feel stuck or face a challenge. Practicing improvisational principles allows you to break free from old patterns and approach life with confidence, creativity, and resilience. One new choice opens the door to unlimited possibilities.

Improv in the Workplace

Improvisation is more than a creativity tool; it is a catalyst for building cognitive flexibility and rapid decision-making, two skills essential for organizational success. Leaders, sales teams, and collaborators who embrace improv principles master real-time problem-solving while making intentional New Choices under pressure. The New Choice framework transforms workplaces into environments where adaptability, innovation, and resilience thrive, empowering individuals and teams to think creatively and act decisively.

How Improv Enhances Decision-Making at Work

The brain rewiring discussed earlier translates directly to workplace environments, strengthening decision-making and adaptability.

Teams trained in the "Yes, And" mindset learn to build on each other's ideas, transforming challenges into opportunities through collaborative thinking.

Improvisation equips professionals to navigate uncertainty with agility, a crucial skill in today's unpredictable business landscape.

Leaders benefit from improv training as it sharpens their ability to identify patterns, explore possibilities, and make bold, informed decisions under pressure. The practice develops intuitive leadership skills that complement analytical capabilities, creating more well-rounded decision-makers.

Leadership Excellence Through Improvisation

Leadership reaches new dimensions through improvisation principles. Leaders who adopt improv techniques become more confident in handling crises, learning to quiet over analysis and trust their instincts when swift action is required. The collaborative nature of improv fosters a culture of innovation, empowering leaders to encourage creative solutions through "Yes, And" thinking.

Improvisation heightens leaders' awareness of team dynamics, enabling them to sense shifts and respond effectively as situations evolve. These enhanced abilities create leaders who are decisive, adaptable, and inspiring qualities that drive organizational success.

Decision-Making in Sales

Due to their high-pressure, dynamic nature, sales environments naturally align with improvisation principles. Sales professionals trained in improvisation develop enhanced abilities to read situations and adjust their approach based on subtle customer cues. Heightened awareness leads to more authentic, unscripted conversations that build genuine trust and rapport.

Improvisation nurtures creativity in negotiation, allowing salespeople to craft innovative solutions that benefit all parties involved. By incorporating the "New Choice" framework into sales strategies, professionals can abandon outdated scripts and focus on creating meaningful, customer-centered experiences. The approach uncovers new opportunities while inspiring teams to think quickly and take purposeful action that strengthens client relationships.

Supporting this connection between creativity and adaptability, Dr. George Land's landmark study for NASA demonstrated that creativity is a learned, and often unlearned, skill. Originally designed to identify innovative problem solvers for NASA's space program, Land's research found that 98% of five-year-olds scored at the "genius" level for creative thinking. By age ten, that number dropped to 30%, and by adulthood, it plummeted to just 2%. The findings revealed that the natural creative capacity we start with erodes over time due to conformity, self-doubt, and overreliance on logic. For sales professionals, this underscores the value of improvisation and the "New Choice" framework as tools to reawaken innate creativity, enhance situational awareness, and strengthen decision-making in the moment.

Decision-Making Through Team Collaboration

Improvisation transforms team dynamics by strengthening bonds and fostering innovation. By building trust through mutual support and shared creativity, improv replaces awkward team-building exercises with authentic connections. Regular practice of New Choices enables teams to respond confidently to unexpected challenges or organizational changes.

The emphasis on adaptability and deliberate action encourages teams to break free from rigid thinking and embrace collaborative ideas that drive progress. When teams integrate the New Choice framework into daily practices, they improve innovation capacity while creating environments where decision-making flows naturally. Improvisation builds trust and adaptability, allowing teams to excel, even under pressure.

Tangible Business Benefits

Improv principles and the New Choice framework generate measurable business outcomes. Flexible mindsets developed through improvisation help employees remain calm and focused during high-stakes situations, reducing stress while increasing success rates. Enhanced mindsets foster employee engagement, as individuals who feel supported and valued are likelier to remain with the organization and contribute meaningfully.

Beyond improving retention, improvisation equips teams with resilience. When setbacks occur, teams trained in improvisation recover quickly and maintain consistent performance. By integrating "New Choice" into decision-making processes, businesses create workplace cultures that thrive on adaptability and innovation. These capabilities enable organizations to respond not just to current challenges but to shape the future with confidence and creativity.

Applying New Choice as a Workplace Practice

The "New Choice" framework provides a practical tool for helping individuals and teams move beyond default responses toward greater adaptability. The process begins with identifying repetitive actions or decisions that no longer align with current goals. Teams can then use "Yes, And" principles to brainstorm fresh, unconventional alternatives while encouraging bold thinking during discussions.

Success depends on rapid implementation. Once teams identify promising alternatives, they should act without hesitation, reinforcing a culture of decisiveness and experimentation.

Following implementation, teams evaluate outcomes, reflect on lessons learned, and refine their approach for future decision-making.

Practicing rapid thinking and intentional "New Choices" transforms hesitation into action, creating workplace cultures where resilience, creativity, and adaptability become natural. Improvisation empowers teams to face challenges confidently while transforming obstacles into opportunities for growth and innovation.

Scene Work:

Take the stage and move from theory to practice with these quick drills to help you catch your defaults, pivot in the moment, and train your brain for change.

- Identify Your Roadblocks: List three psychological barriers that most affect your decisions (fear of failure, perfectionism, self-doubt). Rate each from 1-10 based on how much they impact you.

- Practice "Yes, And" Daily: For five days, when you face frustration or obstacles, acknowledge it ("Yes, this is challenging"), then add a possibility ("And I can try this approach").

- Challenge a Cognitive Bias: Pick one bias (status quo or anchoring) and consciously challenge it in your next decision by asking: "What if I stepped outside my comfort zone?" or "What are three alternatives I haven't considered?"

Side Coaching:

Before making more choices, pause and check in. The following prompts will help you be honest about what's on autopilot and what needs to change.

- Which psychological barriers most affect your ability to make confident decisions?

- What is one default pattern you feel ready to disrupt using "New Choice"?

- How could applying "Yes, And" help you approach current challenges with more curiosity?

Script Revision:

Every rehearsal ends with a new line to carry forward. Try this one on and let it guide your next decision: *I acknowledge my fears and choose courage. Every obstacle is an opportunity to practice new ways of thinking.*

Encore: Choosing To Rewire Your Brain

Decision-making challenges don't reflect personal shortcomings; they reveal how your brain prioritizes survival over clarity. Your neural wiring has kept you safe by scanning for threats, favoring familiar patterns, and clinging to predictable outcomes. However, the exact protective mechanisms that once served you well now create barriers to bold action and innovative thinking.

Improvisation offers a scientifically backed solution to break these cycles. Rather than demanding speed or humor, improv provides practical tools to interrupt mental autopilot. "New Choice" represents a deliberate signal to disrupt habitual loops, training your brain to act without waiting for perfect certainty. "Yes, And" teaches your neural pathways to remain open to possibilities rather than defaulting to resistance.

Neuroscience research confirms that improvisation activates creative brain regions while quieting fear centers, creating optimal conditions for effective decision making. Each application of these principles strengthens new neural pathways, gradually shifting your brain's default from survival to growth.

Transformation occurs through accumulation rather than revelation: hundreds of small pivots, quiet rewiring moments, and instances where you choose experimentation over endless analysis. Forward movement matters more than additional data collection.

Your brain possesses remarkable trainability, and current limitations reflect learned patterns rather than permanent constraints. Every intentional choice is practice for the confident, decisive life you want to create. The capacity for change exists within your neural architecture; improvisation provides the key to unlocking it.

Part Two
Life-Changing Choices

Chapter 4:
Choosing To Rewrite Your Learning Journey

Becoming Knowledgeable in the Moment

"Planning is an unnatural process; it is much more fun to do something." — John Lennon

Education is one of the most powerful tools for transformation, personally, professionally, and globally. Studies show that every additional year of schooling increases income by about 10% worldwide. College graduates, on average, earn over a million dollars more in their lifetime than those with only high school diplomas. The benefits go beyond income. Lifelong learning fuels adaptability in a world that refuses to stand still. It sharpens our minds, strengthens our confidence, and deepens our ability to navigate change.

Research confirms what lived experience often teaches. Education reshapes lives from the inside out. Each additional year of schooling raises global income by roughly 10 percent. College graduates earn over one million dollars more than those with only a high school diploma. These economic gains tell only part of the story. Lifelong learning supports mental agility, stimulates new neural growth, and strengthens the ability to solve complex problems. Consistent learning sharpens memory, expands perspective, and builds emotional intelligence. The ripple effect reaches far beyond individual outcomes. Higher education levels reduce poverty, enhance public health, and foster greater civic participation. Communities with access to education experience lower crime rates and greater economic stability. Global data points to an even broader impact. Each year of education lowers the risk of violent conflict by nearly 20 percent. Learning fuels peace, prosperity, and progress at every level, from personal growth to societal transformation.

On a global scale, education drives economic growth, reduces crime, lowers the risk of conflict, and fosters more engaged communities. Every dollar invested in education yields more than $20 in return. Yet despite its power, access to quality learning remains staggeringly unequal. Over 250 million children are still out of school, and most children in low-income countries can't read by the age of ten. COVID only widened these gaps, pushing millions of students, especially girls and children in low-income areas, further behind.

With stats like these, it's easy to paint education as a guaranteed path to success. The reality is far more nuanced, especially for those who grow up with financial limitations, cultural expectations, or family beliefs that shape what we think is possible.

For many of us, having access to education, especially continuous education, is a privilege. I know how lucky I am. The struggles I encountered while trying to attend college felt painful and unfair at the time. I was constantly navigating the reality of affordability. But looking back, I recognize how fortunate I was compared to others who face even steeper barriers like poverty, discrimination, and systemic inequality.

Growing up, I faced two major hurdles to college. Money was tight, and my dad held traditional views that a woman's place is in the home. I was a natural salesperson even at 16, and I won my dad over with a simple pitch: "What if I were to marry someone who couldn't provide for me and my kids?" Carmie, my dad, saw the logic in that. Looking back, that's a heavy thought for a teenager, but that was my survival instinct kicking in, having grown up with a complicated father figure.

Even though money was tight, I had it better than some, and I was determined to figure it out. In my heart, I knew that earning my degree was my chance to change my financial future. My mantra: turn the impossible into possible. The funny thing is that finding the money for college turned out to be the easiest leg of the journey. The real challenge came with a different set of numbers. Spoiler alert: math and I were never on good terms.

My Learning New Choice Moment

The first and only time I failed a class was during my freshman year. Up until that moment, I had always been a high performer. Failure was not part of my story. Reality sank in as I stared at my grade in Finite Math near the end of the semester. There was no way I was going to pass. My ego refused to accept defeat, and this was not just a matter of pride. I had to pass this class, or my life would be over. Okay, maybe that was a little dramatic - classic 19-year-old logic. Yet in my mind, it was true. Failing meant I could not move on to Calculus, and without Calculus, my carefully planned path to becoming an accountant would crash and burn.

Luckily, I had been resilient and resourceful from a young age because of my challenging upbringing. Giving up was never an option. Others might have quit, but I always asked, "What if?" Long before I understood the power of improv, I had already adopted a mindset of making new choices. Repeating the course was out of the question. It was dreadful, and I could not afford it financially. I had no choice but to throw myself at the mercy of the professor. With confidence, I walked into his office and stated my case. "I need to pass this class to move forward. What are my options?" That was it. A simple ask. He offered me a five-question quiz that would give me just enough points to pass with a D instead of an F.

Sure enough, I passed. Problem solved. Or so I thought.

I felt triumphant and relieved as I walked out of my professor's office, and a bigger problem weighed on me. Math was not just dreadful. I hated it. More importantly, I never even wanted to be an accountant. My moment of elation from passing the class quickly turned into despair and regret. The truth was, I was majoring in accounting to please my father, Carmie.

Carmie was a man who had never finished elementary school, let alone high school or college. He was also very traditional. When I first told him I wanted to go to college, his reaction was, "Why? You will eventually get married and have children. Why waste your time in college? Plus, we do not have the money to send you."

I knew I had to give him a reason that made sense, so I told him that getting a degree was important in case I needed to help support my future family. That reasoning clicked for him. When I was 12, he became very ill and could no longer support his own family. He understood the value of a backup plan. After he accepted my decision to attend college, I felt obligated to pursue his suggestion of becoming an accountant, a career path that seemed both practical and financially secure.

The summer after my first year of college, I felt like I was having a midlife crisis. Paying for 100% of my education meant juggling multiple jobs and piling on student loans, which only added to the pressure. I spent that time intensely reflecting on my options and choices, asking myself what would make me happy while allowing me to repay my loans.

I had always been creative, which led me to wonder if a career in broadcast journalism could be the answer. Ironically, at the age of nine, I auditioned for a television show that mimicked a news

program, but for children. Only now do I realize how deeply that experience had taken root in me. Sadly, the show was canceled before I had the chance to be part of it.

Determined to explore this path, I found a vocational school for radio, television, and film production and met with the career advisor. In that moment, sitting in his office, my future quietly shifted.

As I shared my college concerns and aspirations, the advisor, who later became a close friend, shut his office door and said, "You do not want to come here." He did not explain why, but I later learned the school was not credible. Instead, he suggested I take an improv class at Second City to satisfy my need for a creative outlet.

The next day, I enrolled in my first class. I was the youngest person in the eight-week course, surrounded by professionals with creative careers, most of whom worked for top advertising agencies in Chicago. My classmates became my mentors and most significant influences.

Through that improv class, I discovered my self-worth and natural talents. I became more convinced than ever that I was not designed to be an accountant.

When I returned for my second year of college, I changed my major to journalism. Every weekend, I drove 140 miles round-trip to continue improv classes in the city. By the end of that year, I transferred to a university in downtown Chicago to be closer to improv, career internships, and new opportunities. The deeper I immersed myself in improv, the more I came to embrace the idea of failure. I quickly adapted to making new choices instead of stressing over hard choices.

Decades later, I took another leap and enrolled in a graduate program in organizational leadership. At my age, the decision felt crazy, but it was also exciting and right.

Whether it's a college course or a welding class, choosing to continue learning is never a loss. Every decision to grow through education, in any form, makes us better.

Redefining What It Means to Learn

Failing a math class once felt like the most significant setback of my life. Education had always looked like a straight line to me: work hard, earn the grades, collect the diploma, and walk into a stable career. That belief unraveled when I received a failing grade, not just in the subject, but in the script I thought I had to follow.

The entire framework I had built around education began to unravel when I changed majors. Plans, identity, expectations, and even the definition of success no longer felt fixed. Pressure to prove competence led to a desire to feel a sense of connection to the work. Learning revealed itself as something far more personal than I had ever imagined. No one had taught me to follow energy, to chase what sparked curiosity, or to question whether the plan still served the person I was becoming. Excitement became the new compass. Adaptability replaced rigidity. Letting go of one path created space for something far more aligned to who I really was.

Accounting looked like the responsible choice. I stayed with the major because leaving felt like failure. Permission to pivot opened space for a new direction, one guided by alignment rather than expectation

The setback I feared most became the signal I needed. Failing that class forced an honest conversation with myself. For the first time, I named what I loved. Curiosity pointed me toward journalism, improv, and storytelling. Each choice brought me closer to a career that made sense in terms of how I viewed the world.

The most powerful lessons came outside traditional classrooms. Improv taught me to navigate uncertainty, listen attentively, and create in real-time. Confidence grew from participation, not perfection. Nothing felt scripted, and that felt right.

Psychologist Carol Dweck's research, captured in her book *Mindset: The New Psychology of Success*, reveals that intelligence isn't fixed, and instead grows through challenge, effort, and reflection. Her work reframed how I saw that failed math class. It wasn't proof that I couldn't learn; it was feedback that I needed to learn differently. That idea echoed everything improv had already been teaching me: that mistakes are data, not disasters. The shift from a fixed mindset to a growth mindset transformed not only how I approached education but how I approached life itself.

Returning to graduate school years later brought a different kind of challenge. Balancing ambition, discipline, and doubt required a new level of presence. Even then, the message remained clear. Education lives in every challenge and every decision. No final destination defines success. Growth continues if curiosity stays in the room.

One failed class rewrote my understanding of learning. Rules lost their grip. Curiosity stepped forward. Trust in my instincts laid the groundwork for everything that came next: improv, communication, coaching, leadership, and work that felt fully my own.

No outside force granted permission to begin again. The shift came from choosing to move, even in fear. When the path feels wrong or momentum disappears, growth starts with one decision.

Call "New Choice." Step toward what feels alive. The next version of you is waiting.

The Neuroscience of Learning

Real learning sharpens your mind, not just your resume.

Neuroscience research indicates that engaging in continuous learning can literally keep our brains healthier. It stimulates new neural growth and slows down cognitive decline. Every time we step into unfamiliar territory, whether a new course, a career pivot, or an improv class, we build more than skills; we strengthen our emotional intelligence, confidence, and resilience.

Neuroplasticity allows the brain to adapt through learning. Each new experience, from studying a concept to practicing a skill, strengthens and reshapes neural pathways. Active engagement keeps the brain sharp and supports emotional flexibility. Consistent learning enhances decision-making, stress regulation, and empathy. The process builds more than cognitive function.

Lifelong education lays a strong foundation for mental clarity, emotional strength, and personal growth.

Learning is also how we find our people. Whether in a classroom, a workshop, or a community group, education connects us to others who are also growing and stretching. Learning environments foster a sense of belonging, purpose, and shared momentum.

Redefining what it means to learn means embracing the idea that growth can and should happen at every stage of life. Ultimately, learning is about becoming more of who you are, not just about acquiring knowledge.

Making New Choices in Your Learning: Turning Curiosity into Clarity

Before stepping into a scene on stage, I believed learning was about following directions, earning gold stars, and staying safely within the lines. Structure felt secure. Progress meant finishing assignments, collecting grades, and checking boxes, not exploring what lay beyond them.

Then improv rewrote the rules. On stage, mistakes became momentum. Each misstep invited curiosity instead of correction. Nothing stopped the process unless someone stopped participating. Every choice, right or wrong, built upon the last, propelling the story forward in ways no one could predict. That's when I realized learning isn't about certainty. It's about staying in motion.

Learning follows a similar rhythm as improv. Growth rarely unfolds in a straight line. The clearest direction often reveals itself only after the first step. Action leads to clarity. Confidence develops through engagement, not preparation.

Improvisers embrace this reality. Planning only sets the stage. Growth happens in the response. A scene unfolds one choice at a time. Learning becomes powerful when approached with the same openness and trust.

When progress stalls, improvisers call "New Choice." The moment invites possibility. Changing direction reflects awareness, not weakness. Learners benefit by applying this mindset. Methods, goals, or entire paths can shift. No value exists in remaining on a track that no longer fits.

Failure deserves a reframe. In performance, a missed cue or awkward pause sparks laughter and innovation. Missteps turn into breakthroughs when welcomed. Learning becomes stronger through those exact moments. Mistakes do not diminish growth. They mark the path toward mastery.

Playfulness enhances the process. Pressure alone cannot carry curiosity. Joy, imagination, and freedom unlock deeper understanding. Insight often arrives through experimentation and delight, not just discipline.

Curiosity transforms everything. Each experience offers a chance to explore, adjust, or begin again. Presence matters more than perfection. Learning thrives in our questions, choices, and willingness to stay open as the next scene takes shape.

Ways To Improvise Your Learning in Real Life

Learning goes beyond absorbing information. Shifting perspectives, trying new approaches, and making intentional choices to grow are all essential parts of the process. Earlier in the book, we explored the New Choice improv exercise, which encourages changing direction when something is not working. The same principle applies to learning.

The following exercises will help you rethink your learning path, challenge old beliefs, and step outside your comfort zone. Pick one or try them all, but most importantly, commit to taking action. Growth happens when you choose it.

Scene Work:

- Examine Your Learning Beliefs: Write down three beliefs about education, success, or career stability you grew up with. Ask yourself: "Do these still serve me?" Identify one you want to work on.

- Follow Your Curiosity: Spend 30 minutes this week learning something that genuinely interests you (not because you "should" know it). Notice how different this feels from obligatory learning.

- Redefine Success: Write your current definition of success. Then rewrite it based on who you are now, not who you were when you first chose your path.

Side Coaching:

Before making more choices, pause and check in. The following prompts will help you be honest about what's on autopilot and what needs to change.

- When was the last time you learned something that lit you up because you wanted to, not because you had to?

- What area of your life feels stuck and might be asking for a new approach to growth?

- What would you be curious to explore next if no one else's opinion mattered?

Script Revision:

Every rehearsal ends with a new line to carry forward. Rewrite the script let it guide your next decision:

> *"I am allowed to learn differently, dream differently, and choose again no matter where I started."*

Encore: The Power of Choosing to Learn (Again and Again)

Education reaches far beyond the classroom. Continuous learning begins with a decision.

Finite Math could have ended my journey before it really started. Instead, that moment of panic opened a different direction, built on curiosity, creativity, and alignment. Learning does not follow a straight line. Failure does not signal the end. Changing direction does not mean giving up. Choosing a new path means choosing growth.

Every career change, personal reinvention, or creative risk holds the potential to teach something new. Growth appears when curiosity replaces certainty. Progress happens when flexibility takes the lead. Learning becomes powerful when fueled by presence, courage, and the willingness to begin again.

Exploration creates the classroom. Learning occurs through improvisation, play, and a willingness to look foolish long enough to discover something genuine. Lessons emerge in conversations, unexpected detours, missteps, and breakthroughs. The method matters less than the mindset. The only requirement is choosing to engage.

When the current path no longer fits, academically or otherwise, the next move begins with awareness. A new choice always remains within reach. Real education never asks for perfection; it requires presence. Investing in knowledge, skill, or self-awareness strengthens who you are becoming.

What new direction feels alive right now? Begin before you feel ready. Learn along the way. That is how transformation begins.

Script Notes

You don't need a perfect GPA or permission slip to grow. Use these turning points as inspiration to rethink what learning can look like.

1. Failing My First College Class

My ego hit rock bottom when I bombed Finite Math, but that F taught me more than an A ever could because it was the beginning of questioning my entire direction and rediscovering what I wanted.

2. Begging My Professor for a D

I didn't quit. I asked for options. A straightforward conversation (and a mercy quiz) bought me time and the passing grade I needed. More importantly, it also revealed that I didn't want to be an accountant.

3. Remembering My Nine-Year-Old Dream

A childhood audition for a kids' news show had quietly lived in my memory. That spark led me to explore journalism, reminding me that who we were before life told us who to be still matters.

4. Taking an Improv Class Instead of Switching Schools

A career counselor told me not to attend his school and instead pointed me to Second City. One bold yes led me to improv, a tribe of mentors, and a new way of thinking.

5. Changing My Major (and My City)

After one year of being forced to be an accounting major, I changed to journalism. I transferred to downtown Chicago to be closer to my education: improvement, internships, and opportunity.

6. Driving 140 Miles to Learn Something That Lit Me Up

Every weekend, I commuted to the city for improv. The road trip was long, but so was the list of ways those classes rebuilt my confidence, creativity, and self-worth.

7. Going Back to School as a Grown-Up Woman

Grad school at 50-something wasn't the plan, but I followed it when the fire to lead and grow reignited.

Chapter 5
Choosing Work That Lights You Up

Letting Go of What Looks Good to Do What Feels Right

"The only way to do great work is to love what you do. If you haven't found it yet, keep looking. Don't settle." — Steve Jobs

Career Choices Aren't Just About Paychecks. They're About Power.

Your career shapes more than your résumé. Energy, relationships, identity, and peace of mind all flow from your chosen work. Wrong paths create tension that manifests in your body, bank account, and daily mood. Even when they feel scary or unconventional, the right choices become launchpads for something bigger. Success matters but aligned living transforms everything.

Chasing what looks good on paper but draining your soul is the fastest way to burn out, because alignment matters. When your work aligns with your values, such as freedom, creativity, or purpose, you don't just get paid. You get fulfilled. That ripple effect is real. Fulfillment builds confidence. Confidence fuels momentum. Momentum changes everything. Career choices aren't about climbing a ladder. They're about building a life that feels like yours.

My Career New Choice Moment

I have reinvented my career more times than I have changed my hair color, which is saying something. My journey into career navigation began early, at just 11 years old, reinforcing my belief that kids are among the most fearless risk-takers.

Learning to Hustle at 11 Years Old

My first job was at a flea market, where I worked alongside my father every weekend. I can still smell the musty air in that giant old garage, converted into a bustling maze of vendors selling anything and everything. The environment was gritty and dingy, yet somehow still fun, despite the dreaded 6 a.m. start time. My dad, Carmie, was known as the "Key Man," one of his many pseudonyms. During the week, he worked as a truck driver, both legally for a lighting company and illegally (allegedly) for the mafia. At some point, he even took a home correspondence course to become a locksmith, which later proved to be a more sensible choice given his other activities.

Carmie taught me how to make house and car keys for customers and often left me in charge as the "Key Girl" while he disappeared into the back room for poker games. I quickly learned that adults did not trust a kid to duplicate a key correctly, so I had to prove myself fast. That job taught me how to negotiate, handle money, and, most importantly, experience the power of earning my own money.

My First Career Pivot

One day, another vendor, Joe the Furniture Guy, offered me a job running his booth. The idea of lounging on cushy couches all day made the flea market feel a little less gritty, and the fact that Joe was paying me double what my dad was sealed the deal. It was the first time I had to quit a job and give notice to an employer, though in this case, the employer was my own father.

To my surprise, Carmie respected my decision and released me from my commitment to him. He even agreed to keep driving me to the flea market each weekend. It was my first real lesson in career moves, negotiation, and knowing when to take a better deal.

So many jobs and career pivots followed, each requiring me to adapt and improvise. My background in improv and my ability to stay agile shaped most of those choices.

Saying Yes Before Knowing How

At 23, on a whim, I started my first video production and marketing business. A television sales executive asked if I could produce TV commercials for his clients. I had some production experience but had never run my own business. Still, I said yes, figuring I would figure it out along the way.

Improvisation principles guided this pivotal decision. Stepping on stage unscripted is like starting a business without a solid plan. Trusting the process, building on each moment, and adapting generates momentum that planning alone cannot create. Rather than waiting for complete certainty, I moved forward, leveraged relationships, and adjusted course as needed. The decision sustained me for years, even when success felt far from guaranteed.

Whether starting a business, switching careers, or taking on a leadership role, the key is to start before you feel ready. Improvisers do not get the luxury of preparation. They step into uncertainty with confidence and adaptability. That same mindset can transform how you approach career decisions. That lesson carried over when I faced my next unexpected career challenge. This time, it was in an industry in which I had never imagined myself.

From Film to Finance: Running an IMAX Theater

Then came the job offer to manage an IMAX theater. I had production and business experience, but this situation was different in terms of scale and complexity. I'd be overseeing everything, including accounting, which was ironic, since I'd once flunked out of it as a major.

At first, I kept turning it down. The role felt massive. The recruiter mentioned the salary, and I was in. I said yes and figured out how to manage a publicly traded operation on the fly.

That job led to another IMAX role in a new city. Then the economy tanked, and the position vanished. Two decades of pivoting, leading, and white knuckling through imposter syndrome caught up with me. The burnout was real. I needed something different.

Burnout and a New Direction

Miserably burned out, I asked myself when I had been happiest. The answer came quickly. Improv classes have always brought me joy due to their therapeutic aspect. Clinging to that realization, I searched for an improv class in my new city, only to discover that none existed. The realization crushed me. Someone suggested I start my improv community. It was the last thing I wanted, but I could not ignore the "Yes And" mindset. Saying no would have made me a hypocrite.

Carolina Improv Company was born. I leveraged my marketing, operations, and entertainment experience to build a brand while seeking guidance on how to instruct. I knew how to improvise but had never been an instructor, which probably explained my hesitation. Juggling this new venture with a full-time job felt like chaos, but I refused to stop.

One week before my first class was set to begin, I was terminated from IMAX. I had four students, a stack of business cards, and no job. I had improvised my way into an improv career I had never planned. Somehow, everything had come full circle.

Losing Everything and Reinventing Again

When COVID arrived, it shut down my theater and corporate training business in one swift and painful blow. At the same time, I was going through a divorce, had no income, and was dangerously close to hitting rock bottom. Everything I had worked so hard to build was falling apart at the same time.

Losing the business was like watching a home I had carefully constructed collapse piece by piece. Every decision had been intentional, and every part of it carried meaning. I believed dedication, purpose, and a strong foundation would be enough to keep it standing. When it all fell apart, I stood there questioning the plan I had followed and whether the version of success I pursued ever truly fit.

Out of necessity, I accepted a job selling life insurance. I didn't enjoy it and wasn't sure I would succeed, but I needed a way forward. Then I heard a competitor was hiring sales trainers.

Training always brought me to life, so I decided to take a chance and make the call.

He was surprised. I was transparent. I told him, "My business is barely staying afloat. I don't have the resources to keep it going."

He said yes.

One decision opened the door, allowing me to begin again with greater clarity, profound courage, and a renewed sense of purpose.

Rebuilding with Experience and Passion

After three years of closure, I restarted the theater on a smaller scale while continuing my work with the sales training company. Over time, I rebuilt the business with a deeper level of experience, particularly in sales. Along the way, I also discovered a passion for organizational leadership and development, which led me to pursue graduate school. Through every career shift, improv has been the constant thread that has helped me adapt, grow, and thrive.

How Improv Helped Me Reinvent, Rebuild, and Rise

Improv had been preparing me for reinvention long before I knew I'd need it. Its core principles (trust the process, stay present, and build on whatever shows up) became my survival guide for starting over. Every pivot in my career, from producing videos to managing an IMAX theater to becoming a corporate sales trainer, followed those same rules.

My boldest career moves always came before I felt qualified. At twenty-three, I launched a video production company without formal business training. Years later, I accepted a corporate sales training role with minimal sales training experience. Each leap terrified me, but hesitation would have cost me momentum. Improv taught me to step forward even when the plan wasn't clear, to say "Yes, And" to the unknown.

Improvisation reshaped how I approached uncertainty. On stage, you don't wait until you're ready. Instead, you start, listen, adapt, and find your footing in real time. The same is true in life. Confidence doesn't come from preparation alone; it comes from participation. Progress happens in motion, not in waiting for permission.

Embracing Uncertainty with Confidence

My career began at eleven, when I cut keys at a flea market, and later evolved into creating an improv company in a city that lacked one. None of it followed a master plan. Presence mattered more than perfect planning. You move forward without clarity, trusting the path will form as you walk it.

Beyond Scripts: Building Authentic Connection

Whether selling television advertisements, marketing educational programs, or leading corporate trainings, improvisation fundamentally transformed my approach. Presence proved more potent than pressure tactics. Authentic conversations generated better results than any rehearsed pitch.

"Yes, And" principles converted discovery calls from scripted monologues into collaborative dialogues. Clients experienced genuine engagement rather than transactional exchanges. Every interaction became an opportunity to co-create solutions that served everyone involved.

Redefining Rejection

Rejection used to feel personal until I learned otherwise through improv. A failed scene simply signals a new beginning, and a "no" indicates a shift, not an ending. Instead of retreating, I learned to ask better questions and follow the next cue. Every setback became another chance to pivot and play again. Building that resilience made forward momentum unstoppable.

Leading with Creative Fire

Improvisation unlocked my creative edge. Bold ideas stopped hiding and began to shine. Whether launching a new business or cutting through sales noise, my whole personality came through. Energy shifted, and momentum followed. Leaning into what made me different drew people in faster and more deeply. Creativity became my differentiator.

Passion Finds Its Way Back

Improvisation remained a constant thread throughout my career, even when I wasn't actively practicing. Every professional role I embraced, such as coach, educator, salesperson, and leader, carried its influence forward. Passion requires no formal title or designated space; it simply needs permission to infuse the work that matters most.

One Big, Evolving Scene

Every chapter builds on the last. I didn't abandon my past; I repurposed it. Improv moved from the stage to the boardroom, from comedy to corporate strategy. My career has never followed a straight line, but the constant has been my willingness to choose again.

Waiting for certainty keeps momentum frozen. The next move doesn't require readiness; authenticity matters more. Careers don't follow ladders; they follow creativity. When a situation feels stale, step forward. Choose again. Let courage lead, and clarity follow.

Ways To Improvise Your Career With Power & Purpose

You don't need a five-year plan. You need five seconds of courage and one bold move. Improv doesn't wait for perfect conditions, and neither should you.

Scene Work:

Take the stage and move from theory to practice with these quick drills to help you catch your defaults, pivot in the moment, and train your brain for change.

- **Say Yes Before You're Ready:** Apply for one role you're curious about (even if you don't check every box), volunteer for a stretch project, or take one bold step toward a side project this week.

- **Reframe Failure as Feedback:** Write about one career "failure" or setback. List three ways it made you stronger or redirected you toward something better.

- **Build with "Yes, And":** In one work conversation this week, validate someone's idea before offering your perspective. Notice how this shifts the energy and collaboration.

Side Coaching:

Before making more choices, pause and check in. The following prompts will help you be honest about what's on autopilot and what needs to change.

- Where are you staying safe instead of taking a chance in your career?
- What's one career path you've secretly wanted but never tried?
- What would you attempt next if you didn't have to be perfect?

Script Revision:

Every rehearsal ends with a new line to carry forward. Rewrite the script and let it guide your next decision:

"I don't need a script to move forward. I say yes with courage, build as I go, and step into work that fits who I'm becoming."

Encore: Real Careers Are Built Like Flea Markets

Careers begin like flea markets: messy, unpredictable, and full of unexpected discoveries. Something magical happens within that maze of vendors, rusted tools, and hidden treasures. People find what they never knew they were looking for.

My career never followed a traditional blueprint. From duplicating keys at eleven to designing leadership strategies for corporate executives, each move required improvisation over preparation. Success came from saying yes before feeling ready, then building competence through action rather than analysis.

Improvisation transforms career navigation from survival mode into creative expression. Traditional career advice suggests mapping every step before moving. Improv wisdom suggests the opposite: movement creates the map. Direction emerges through engagement, not endless planning.

Careers don't require day-one clarity; they require sustained momentum. Purpose reveals itself through experimentation, not meditation. Growth happens when you choose action over certainty, curiosity over comfort, and possibility over perfection.

Every vendor at that old flea market started with an empty table and a willingness to see what would sell. Some failed spectacularly, while others discovered gold mines in forgotten corners. They all learned something valuable about showing up consistently, adapting quickly, and trusting the process.

Your career operates the same way. Set up your booth, display your talents boldly, and trust that customers will find you when you offer something genuine and valuable. You're not starting from scratch. You're choosing again, with accumulated wisdom, refined instincts, and unshakeable confidence in creating something meaningful from whatever materials you have.

The next chapter of your career is waiting. Stop planning and start building.

Script Notes: Reinventing My Career Without a Map

Use these career pivots as inspiration for your next move. You don't need a perfect plan. You just need one bold moment of clarity and courage.

1. **Quitting My Dad for a Couch Gig**

At 11, I left my flea market job with my dad to work for the furniture guy who paid double. It was my first lesson in negotiation, value, and not letting guilt keep me in the wrong role.

2. **Starting a Business Without a Business Plan**

At 23, I launched a video production company without knowing how to run one. I said yes before I knew how and figured it out on the fly. Making that decision taught me that momentum matters more than mastery.

3. **Saying Yes to a Job I Kept Turning Down**

Managing an IMAX theater sounded ridiculous for someone who had failed as an accounting major, but I said yes to the salary and stayed for the lesson in self-trust and scale.

4. **Teaching Improv Without Ever Teaching Before**

I didn't want to start an improv company. I especially didn't want to teach, but when there were no classes in my city, I built what I wished existed. That first "Yes, And" became the start of something huge.

5. **Getting Fired the Week I Launched a New Business**

IMAX let me go before I started teaching my first class. With only four students and no paycheck, I improvised my way into a career I hadn't planned but was unknowingly built for.

6. **Saying Goodbye to a Dream, Hello to a Lifeline**

COVID crushed my business. I could've gone back to bartending if the restaurants weren't forced to shut down. Instead, I said yes to selling insurance and then landed a job as a corporate trainer, where I finally got paid to do what I love.

Chapter 6

Choosing Your Financial Truth Confidently

Ditching Guilt, Owning Worth, and Making Money Moves That Stick

"You must gain control over your money or the lack of it will forever control you." — Dave Ramsey

Writing about my financial hardships is both painful and oddly liberating. Most people I know struggle with this topic, especially in partnerships, whether marriage or business. At one point, I was on track to become an accountant, and now I have a lot of friends in that world. One of them described finance as "being in someone's financial underwear drawer." That visual has never left me. Just the thought of someone rifling through my metaphorical privates drawer sparks instant fear of judgment and a strong urge to hide under the bed.

Fear of judgment and shame kept me from writing this chapter. Over time, I've learned to wear my financial failures like Girl Scout badges, but I still have those "What the hell was I thinking?" moments. When that shame spiral kicks in, I remind myself: those moments were just the cost of tuition for a life lesson.

Before I fling open my financial drawer and procrastinate a little longer, I want to share what I've learned about why talking about money makes so many of us squirm. According to the American Psychological Association, 72% of adults admit they feel stressed about money at least occasionally, with 22% feeling extremely stressed. The underlying fear is often the same: people will think we're clueless about money.

Plenty of other reasons keep us from taking control of our finances. Shame. Guilt. Cultural taboos. Emotional baggage. Lack of education. Power struggles. Pride. Fear of looking greedy. Avoidance. Comparison. That nasty little voice that whispers, "You should be further along," or "Why can't you be like her?"

Each of those boxes has had a checkmark next to my name.

My drawer holds more than a few ugly little financial gems, but I'm choosing to share the two moments that leveled me. These were not just inconvenient setbacks. These were ground-shaking, gut-wrenching, make-you-question-your-worth moments.

The remarkable transformation: those same devastating moments now serve as sources of inspiration and strength. When asked about my most significant accomplishments, both financial disasters would easily rank in my top five achievements.

The Con Artist Comeback

At 28, I was living my best life in the first home I bought on my own when I met a man at church. The setup sounds like a bad Lifetime movie, right?

After everything unfolded, I was interviewed on Court TV for a segment about sweetheart swindlers. Other producers reached out too, wanting my story for their shows. After telling it once, the shame hit hard and kept crashing. That shame stuck around. I honestly believe it's one of the reasons it took me so long to write my first book. As I type this now, tears still threaten to rise. The memory still stings.

During that season, I was building a career, climbing ladders, doing everything I thought I should do. Despite all of it, I felt hollow. Grief for my dad lingered. He had passed six years earlier.

We were close, and without him, something always felt missing. My relationship with my mom was rocky at best, and my dad had been my grounding force.

To feel close to him again, I started going to church. Not just any church. His church. The place where he was baptized. The one where we sat together every Christmas. The same one that later held his memorial service.

That church is also where I met Dean, also known as Dino.

He was small in stature, but funny and charismatic. His claim that he knew my dad pulled me in the most. That intrigued me. Carmie, my father, allegedly worked for the Italian mafia. He was not a famous name, but apparently well-known behind the scenes. From what I've been told, he allegedly worked as a driver for one of Chicago's biggest bosses, Sam Giancana.

Dean shared details only a few people would have known. He even had a coin that matched one from my dad's collection. That coin felt like a breadcrumb from Carmie himself, and I followed it.

Dean posed as someone who had come into my life for a reason. He was not just a charming guy I met at church. He was a practiced con artist. I was one of his many marks.

He studied me, said the right things, played the long game, and earned my trust. We became a couple, talked about marriage, and set a wedding date at the very church where we met.

Soon after, he began sharing stories about mob threats and unpaid debts. He never asked for money directly at first. I volunteered to help. I paid for lawyers. I paid for protection. I paid for peace of mind.

The New Choice Effect

Eventually, the well ran dry. That is when Dean started asking for money. According to him, we could not get married until everything was resolved. My life, he said, was in danger. People were watching me, following me.

I panicked. For him. For my family. For myself.

I started cash-advancing credit cards, selling personal belongings, and stopping paying bills, including the mortgage. I went into a tailspin.

The madness ended when I found out I was not his only target. At least two other women were tangled in his web.

There is much more to that story; maybe someday I will tell it all. For now, here is what matters: I never got my money back, and I never got justice. Instead of arresting Dean, the police officers filed my claim as a civil complaint to pursue on my own.

The emotional fallout was brutal. My family cut me off. Judgment replaced support. I had no choice but to rebuild my life, alone.

Crawling Out from Under the Crumbled Facade

The numbers are a blur now. Trauma does that. Still, I remember watching my credit card debt creep toward thirty thousand dollars, money I'd advanced to Dean in the name of our "future." That figure doesn't even include all the other payments I made trying to hold it all together.

Survival has always been my muscle memory. I learned it early. My dad was on disability, and we lived off Social Security and whatever he could earn at the flea market. There were no safety nets, just hustle. When college said no to financial aid, I said yes to every side job that could keep me there. That scrappiness became my degree in resilience.

After graduation, when the economy collapsed and jobs disappeared, I didn't wait for opportunity to knock; I built the door. Out of necessity, I started my first business. By twenty-five, I'd bought a multi-unit property even though every banker and real estate agent told me I couldn't. That defiance wasn't ego, it was survival dressed as courage.

So when everything with Dean imploded, those same survival instincts kicked in again. Losing the money hurt. Losing my first property cut like a knife. Losing my self-trust cut deeper. But the girl who'd hustled her way through college and bought property against the odds wasn't gone. She just had to claw her way back.

Step one: I placed an ad for a roommate to cover the mortgage.

Step two: I stacked jobs, being a publicist by day, cocktail waitress by night. My life sounded like a country song, minus the pickup truck.

Step three: I picked up the phone and called every credit card company I owed. There was no script, just honesty. I told them I'd been conned, and they could either settle or get nothing if I filed for bankruptcy. Every single one agreed.

The hotel where Dean had been living in secret had charged my card for his stay without my permission. When the manager called, the truth unraveled. I threatened legal action if they didn't reverse the charges, and they did. That moment changed me. I found my voice again, one call at a time.

The last step was letting go of my home. I sold it on my own terms to pay off additional debt, moved to downtown Chicago, and started over. I wasn't just rebuilding; I was reclaiming. Even with charge-offs, my credit rebounded quickly. I became debt-free, independent, and eventually bought another property.

That chapter became my blueprint for reinvention. Every mistake turned into fuel. Every fear became a lesson.

I stopped seeing money as a threat and started treating it like a skill, like improv or riding a bike. Once you figure it out, you can always figure it out again.

And I would need that truth to carry me through the next test life had waiting.

The Covid Conquest

Lessons from the Dean disaster were no longer abstract. They lived in my bones. The survival experience created a foundation I could stand on when the next storm hit. A global pandemic collided with a failing marriage and a business in free fall. There was no outside villain, no scandal, just real-world chaos moving in all at once.

Nothing sharpens your negotiation skills like staring down a mountain of debt and realizing you must sell your house to survive. The mess with Dean forced me to juggle credit cards, let go of a home I loved, and stay afloat under pressure. I came out stronger. Financially. Mentally. Emotionally. Creatively.

One of the biggest lessons I took from that time was the power of asking. Whether help, a payment extension, or a better deal is needed, asking matters. The odds are fifty-fifty. You either get a yes or a no. Not asking guarantees a no. I stopped leaving opportunities on the table.

Facing my next crisis, I already knew how to escape a financial mess. What I lacked was confidence in building long-term stability. Years of shame had buried that belief. My dad retired when I was twelve. We lived on Social Security and flea market hustle. Our family survived through grit and street smarts. Energy like that shaped me.

When everything fell apart with Dean, my improv training helped me think on my feet. I asked "what if?". I imagined new scenarios. I picked up the phone and negotiated from scratch. No one taught me that. I invented it from necessity.

Later, I moved cities, landed a new job, got married, and the pandemic hit. My theater business shut down. Revenue disappeared. Divorce laws forced me to live separately from my soon-to-be ex. No income. No safety net. Sixty-five thousand dollars in credit card debt. This was even worse than the Con Artist Chaos.

Experience had given me tools. I asked the questions again: What if I called? What if I got creative?

Shortly after the divorce, I met my now-husband. We shared the same goal: no debt before marriage. We enrolled in Financial Peace University through our church. The decision changed everything. Dave Ramsey's program didn't just teach us about money; it taught us about intentionality. His core principle, that you must gain control over your money or the lack of it will forever control you, applies to every area of life. The same discipline required to follow Ramsey's "snowball method" is what "New Choice" demands: stop making decisions on autopilot and start choosing with purpose.

Credit card interest was draining my money faster than savings could grow. I stopped playing it safe and started attacking the debt. Every spare dollar went toward balances. Over time, the numbers shrank. Within a year, they were gone.

Debt-free felt unreal. The feeling didn't last long. Another question popped up: what about retirement?

With nothing saved, I leaned into the hustle. A sales job allowed me to earn big when things went well and save for lean months. Learning to ride those income waves taught me discipline.

With the guidance of a financial planner, we began to build a successful retirement strategy.

Everything circled back to the same toolkit: creativity, resourcefulness, and the power of asking.

Why We Get Stage Fright with Financial Choices

Money touches every aspect of our lives, yet it is one of the most emotionally charged topics we tend to avoid discussing. For many, financial decisions are driven not by logic but by fear, guilt, shame, or outdated narratives that have been inherited from family or society. Whether you were taught that money is hard to come by, that talking about it is taboo, or that you must hold onto every dollar "just in case," those beliefs create emotional roadblocks that shape how you spend, save, and earn.

Much like improvisation, financial choices often require us to respond to the unexpected. The problem is, we tend to freeze when the unexpected shows up. Our brains are wired for certainty, and financial uncertainty can be a threat. So, we default. We keep the same budget, which doesn't work. We avoid looking at our bank accounts. We say yes to work that underpays us because we fear losing what little we think we have.

Calling "New Choice" on these patterns requires us to see money not as a fixed outcome, but as a flexible tool: a relationship we can evolve. In this moment, improvisation becomes an unexpected but powerful ally.

How Improv Helped Me Rebalance My Checkbook

Improv is the toolkit that has carried me through some of the hardest financial seasons of my life. When everything felt like falling apart, I leaned into the same skills I use on stage: presence, flexibility, and the courage to call "new choice." Improv taught me how to:

Pivot without a script

Financial disaster requires improvisation, plus strategy. After the con, I contacted every creditor armed with transparency and courage. Raw honesty replaced polished presentations. Genuine conversations and bold requests opened doors that seemed permanently closed.

Vulnerability and determination erased the debt that once felt insurmountable.

Trade shame for movement

Financial shame tried to keep me quiet, and improv taught me to stay in motion. Selling my house wasn't a failure. Starting over in a mobile home wasn't a defeat. Those were simply scene changes. I kept moving forward, one dollar at a time.

Solve creatively under pressure

When the pandemic collided with a divorce and a business collapse, I didn't crumble. Improv had already trained me to find the next move when the plan vanished. I made choices that seemed insignificant in the moment but ultimately led to significant shifts over time.

Rewrite the money story

I stopped seeing money as mysterious or shameful. It became a relationship I could learn, a language I could speak. Like improv, money is about presence, choice, and practice. Every time I chose clarity over chaos, I got stronger.

You might wonder what improv techniques I deployed to navigate my financial chaos with creativity, presence, and power. Here's how they showed up, Gina-style:

"Yes, And"

I accepted what was real (debt, betrayal, zero safety net) and moved forward.

Yes, I got conned. And I can still make the next smart move.

Yes, I'm embarrassed. And I'm still picking up the phone.

New Choice

When the scene stalls in improv, I call "new choice" repeatedly.

- When creditors didn't respond? New script.
- When shame screamed "hide"? New energy.
- When my house felt more like a trap than a triumph? I ended the scene.

Make Strong Offers

Improv made me braver and taught me to make specific, confident offers. I stopped waiting for permission and started boldly asking for grace periods, payment plans, and clarity from banks and landlords. Curiosity replaced fear, and sometimes, the answers surprised me. I negotiated like a woman who knew my value, even when I was close to bankruptcy.

Stay in the Scene

Improv teaches presence. I stayed present with the discomfort, the numbers, the fear. I didn't numb out or "exit stage left." I stayed in it, even when it hurt, and made micro-moves forward.

Play to the Top of Your Intelligence

I didn't play small. I researched. I learned. I called in my accountant, my negotiator, and my hustler. I used every ounce of intelligence, instinct, and emotional agility to climb out.

Listen Fully

Improv requires listening to others, to the scene, and yourself. I stopped reacting out of panic and started responding from the truth. I heard the fear, but didn't let it direct my script.

Trust the Ensemble

Eventually, I allowed trusted people in, like my now-husband, a financial planner, and my new church community. I didn't try to solo my way through Act III. I built a better cast.

Improvisation skills were my survival tactics, and not abstract concepts. I made financial recovery an improvised art, and now I'm giving others the script rewrite they need.

Exercises For Your Financial Debut

Scene Work:

Take the stage and move from theory to practice with these quick drills to help you catch your defaults, pivot in the moment, and train your brain for change.

- Track and Reframe: Track one financial habit for seven days (spending, saving, or earning). Then reframe one limiting money belief using "Yes, And" (e.g., "Yes, I've made mistakes with money, and I can learn better habits").

- Make a Low-Risk Financial Pivot: Choose one small area where you can shift your money habits: start a savings automation, negotiate one bill, or have an honest conversation about finances with yourself or a trusted person.

- Create a Money Momentum Plan: Build a simple budget or money map using any tool that works for you. Focus on progress, not perfection. Celebrate small wins.

Side Coaching:

Before making more choices, pause and check in. The following prompts will help you be honest about what's on autopilot and what needs to change.

- What emotions or memories surface when you think about money?

- What default financial habits or beliefs might be holding you back?

- What is one small financial "New Choice" you can make this week?

Script Revision:

Every rehearsal ends with a new line to carry forward. Rewrite the script and let it guide your next decision:

"Financial freedom is a decision, not a fantasy. I trade guilt for grit and create something better by taking intentional action."

Encore: New Choice, New Currency

Financial honesty creates the foundation for every other choice you want to make. Clarity replaces chaos when you face what's happening with your money (what's coming in, what's going out, and what patterns are sabotaging your progress). Avoidance might feel safer temporarily, but it compounds stress over time. Bills don't disappear. Debt doesn't shrink through denial. Taking control gives you options, whether eliminating debt, building emergency funds, or investing with intention.

Financial awareness breaks destructive cycles. Emotional spending loses its power. Lifestyle inflation stops driving decisions. One conscious choice builds momentum for the next. Over time, intentional actions create stability, improve creditworthiness, and expand future possibilities.

The most profound transformation happens internally. When you stop running from your financial reality, shame loses its grip. Fear diminishes. Self-acceptance emerges. You recognize that numbers tell only part of your story. Resilience, creativity, and determination write the rest. Change extends beyond bank accounts to emotional and spiritual growth, building unshakeable self-trust.

Improvisation teaches you to work with present conditions rather than waiting for perfect circumstances. You show up with what you have. You listen to what's needed. You pivot when necessary. You call "New Choice" and create something better in real time.

Financial presence becomes the catalyst that breaks you free from old patterns.

Survival mode no longer defines your relationship with money. You're steering toward freedom, agency, and a future where bank statements don't trigger anxiety. You meet financial reality with confidence and declare, "New Choice! I've got this." Tomorrow, you repeat it because financial wellness is an ongoing improvisation, and you're already mastering the scene.

Your financial story isn't finished. Every day presents another opportunity to choose differently, spend intentionally, and build the stability that supports your most ambitious dreams. The stage is set. Your next scene starts now.

These are the financial choices that redefined my relationship with money. Use them as fuel to spark your own new choice moments.

Script Notes: Rewriting My Financial Story

These moments helped me regain control of my financial story through truth-telling, bold boundaries, and refusing to let shame drive the narrative. Let them inspire your New Choice moments, where you stop surviving money stress and start rewriting your future with intention.

1. **Naming the Scam Out Loud**

After months of silence and shame, I said the words: "I was conned." That truth set me free. Denial keeps you stuck. Ownership gets you unstuck.

2. **Calling Every Creditor Without a Script**

I picked up the phone, told the truth, and negotiated from scratch. There was no perfection, just presence. Every call rebuilt my confidence and erased my fear.

3. **Stacking Jobs Without Shame**

Publicist by day, cocktail waitress by night. That grind wasn't beneath me. It was a bridge. I chose hustle over helplessness and built my comeback one tip at a time.

4. **Letting Go of the House on My Terms**

I didn't sell in panic. I sold in power. I waited until I could choose it, not collapse into it. That decision felt like reclaiming my future.

5. **Turning Financial Pain into Improv Power**

I used the tools I taught on stage: "yes, and," "new choice," and bold offers to navigate debt, doubt, and big, scary decisions. Survival became a strategy.

6. **Saying No to Debt Before Saying Yes to Love**

Before remarrying, I committed myself: I wouldn't carry old debt into new love. That boundary became a promise I kept, and it changed everything.

7. **Writing a New Script for Retirement**

No trust fund. No early inheritance. Just clarity, curiosity, and a financial planner who got me. We built a retirement plan from the ground up with improvisation and intention.

Chapter 7

Choosing To Create a Healthy Home

Curating Spaces That Reflect Who You're Becoming

"A true home is one of the most sacred of places. It is a sanctuary into which men flee from the world's perils and alarms."
— *J.R. Miller*

Choosing a home environment means more than picking the correct zip code or granite countertops. Home should reflect your identity, support your growth, and protect your peace. That doesn't come from a floor plan. It comes from intention.

No one path defines what home looks like. Mine has zigzagged through every kind of living situation imaginable. Every choice and pivot came from a gut-level decision to trust myself. Improvisation became my secret weapon. Not the stage kind with jazz hands, although those have appeared. Real-life improv, the type that shows up when you hit a wall and choose your next move anyway.

Why Home Matters So Much to Me

Calm didn't exist in my childhood home. My mother drank heavily. I didn't have the words for addiction back then. The emotional instability screamed louder than she did. My father, though kind and steady, stayed silent. That silence protected her and abandoned the rest of us.

One night, my brother cracked under the pressure. He threatened to end his life. I snapped and finally called the situation what it was. I told my mother she was an alcoholic. My father looked me in the eye and told me to apologize.

That moment told me everything. Creating a safe space of my own had to become a priority. That choice marked one of my earliest "New Choice" moments. Instead of sticking to the script my family kept repeating, I rewrote the scene and took my first step toward emotional independence.

The College Apartment That Saved My Sanity

Freedom came in the form of college. My half-sister helped me financially and insisted I get out. That first step into independence shifted everything.

After transferring schools and returning to the city, I returned home to save money. That decision came with a cost. The tension reignited. One night, while I studied at the dining room table, my mom stumbled out of the bedroom, irritated by the light. "When are you moving out, college girl?" she slurred.

Right then, I decided. "Two weeks," I said. I had no money or plan, just needed to get out. That moment stood out as an apparent "New Choice." I didn't need the details. I needed a deadline.

Grabbing the newspaper, I scanned the rental listings and found a $375 attic apartment near the airport. The space was cramped and hot with no air conditioning. Still, it became my sanctuary. Peace arrived for the first time in years.

The First House and the Power of Instant Decisions

My early twenties were spent working in TV and film. Colleagues, mostly older and seasoned, gave me solid advice. "Buy property," they said. I didn't want a condo. I wanted a multi-unit building where I could live in one unit and rent out the others.

Every real estate agent I spoke with tried to talk me out of it. One asked, "What will you do when the water heater breaks?" My answer: "Same thing you do. Call someone and write a check."

That kind of certainty came from years of improv. Weekly practice taught me how to trust my instincts and respond without panic. Investing in something no one thought I could handle became another powerful "New Choice." I didn't wait for approval. I trusted my gut and moved forward.

Eventually, I found a young loan officer who worked hard to make my loan happen. Later, he told me I was his first client. He still believed in possibility, and so did I.

The Rollercoaster of Real Estate and Relationships

After that first house, I flipped a few more. Some were profitable, and others, not so much. The 2008 crash took a toll. That same year, I moved to a new city with my then-fiancé. We rented while I held onto my Chicago dream home, convinced I'd return someday.

The IMAX job I relocated for eventually disappeared, but the bills didn't. Selling the Chicago house became my lifeline. The money went toward building a different kind of home: a improv theater.

In 2009 I opened the theater and announced to our first audience: "Make yourselves at home because you're sitting in my Chicago condo." Naming the theater after one I loved back home, Uptown Theater, gave me something familiar to hold onto. Letting go of yet another home became a powerful new choice. Making that move redirected my energy for more transformation.

The marriage ended. We never bought a house together. He didn't want to, and maybe he didn't really want the marriage either.

That realization became its own quiet new choice. I stopped compromising with people who didn't want to build anything real.

From Mobile Home to Real Home

During my marital separation, I temporarily moved into a mobile home. It was not fancy, but it was definitely mine. I made it cozy. Then I moved again. And again. Each space became a new version of home. Each move gave me another chance to reset, both emotionally and physically.

When I met my now-husband, we agreed early on that we would buy together. There would be no more renting, no more temporary setups.

We searched in a tough market with low inventory. A builder entered the picture. Loan officers hesitated due to my commission-based income. We kept going. After a few failed starts, we found the right team and finally got the green light. That entire process felt like a living improv scene. Every obstacle became a new choice opportunity to pivot, reframe, and move forward.

Now I'm writing this chapter from the house we built. Every inch of it was earned and cherished.

Why Your Home Environment Matters (More Than You Think)

Where you live doesn't just hold your stuff. It holds your nervous system. Your home shapes how you feel, how you function, and how you show up.

Let's get into it:

Your Body Feels Everything

Clean air, safe water, and functional space are not luxuries. They're essentials. Poor environments increase stress, especially for kids. That stress becomes chronic illness, inflammation, or burnout. Your body reflects your surroundings.

Your Mind Reacts Instantly

A peaceful space brings focus, while a chaotic one keeps your brain in defense mode. Light, order, and intention lower anxiety and restore clarity, and a clear space builds a clear mind.

Your Energy Teaches People How to Treat You

Home is where emotional patterns form. Kids learn what a safe connection feels like. Adults either recharge or unravel. Supportive conversation and emotional safety shape how everyone in the house shows up in the world.

Your Space Should Feel Like You

The right environment helps you breathe deeper. Personal touches and meaningful objects create alignment. When your space reflects your values, you move through the world more rooted.

Your Resources Shape Your Options

Not everyone has equal access to quality housing. Socioeconomic status affects health outcomes. The system is broken when families are forced to choose between affordability and safety; naming the issue is part of the solution.

How you live directly affects how you lead, relate, and recover. Your home doesn't have to be perfect. It needs to be aligned. Choose that on purpose.

How Improv Built My Home Life (and Can Build Yours)

Improv taught me how to navigate the unexpected. Home has never been a fixed address in my life. Instead, it's been a series of pivots. Each one required a decision made on the spot, with limited information and zero guarantees. That's improv.

When the script collapsed, I didn't freeze. I made a new choice. When the plan changed, I adapted. Not perfectly. Not painlessly. But consistently. The lessons of improv became muscle memory.

Here's how improv skills can help you build a better home life, whether that's where you live or how you live in it:

- Trust the first offer. Improv trains you to follow your instincts. That attic apartment near the airport? It wasn't fancy, but it was freedom. Improv helps you distinguish between a fear-based choice and a forward-moving one.

- Make the move before the plan is perfect. In improv, waiting too long to make a move kills the scene. Same with life. You don't need all the answers before you say yes to change.

- Reframe the scene, not the truth. Improv is about redirection. When my job disappeared, the sale of my house became a theater. I wasn't spinning a story. I was rewriting it with a purpose.

- Say yes, then figure it out. Building a home with David, my husband, wasn't linear. Loan issues, market madness, and personal history all showed up. We responded in real time, together, one yes at a time.

- Honor what the space means to you. A home isn't defined by square footage. Instead, it's defined by what it lets you become. Improv gave me the language for that.

If life has taught you to expect chaos, improv teaches you how to breathe inside and helps you build something grounded, even when everything is in the air. You don't need perfect conditions to create peace. You just need presence, practice, and the power to say, "new choice."

Design Your Home Space Like an Improviser

In improv, we teach an exercise called "Build a Room." Students create an entire space in their imagination. They place furniture, hang artwork, and choose the lighting, all without a single prop. Then, they perform a scene inside that invisible room, honoring what everyone else created. No one walks through a couch or ignores a lamp because the space has been made real through commitment. When done well, the audience sees everything. Their imaginations light up because the improvisers fully commit to the world they built.

Purposeful environments generate this shift naturally.

Your real-life space deserves the same care. It's more than walls and furniture. It's an extension of you. How you live inside it shapes your nervous system, creativity, and clarity. You don't need a remodel. Try these improv-inspired moves to redesign your home environment with intention:

Scene Work:

Take the stage and move from theory to practice with these quick drills to help you catch your defaults, pivot in the moment, and train your brain for change.

- Walk Your Space Like a Scene: Move through your home as if seeing it for the first time. Make a list of what drains your energy and what sparks peace. Choose one area to shift.

- "Yes, And" Your Space: Pick one cluttered or joyless area and transform it with a small but meaningful change: clear a surface, add lighting, or create a dedicated space for something you love.

- Recast a Room's Purpose: Identify one room or corner that needs a new role. Could your dining table become a creativity station? Turn one space into what you actually need it to be.

Side Coaching:

Before making more choices, pause and check in. The following prompts will help you be honest about what's on autopilot and what needs to change.

- What does "home" feel like to you right now, and what do you want it to feel like?

- Which part of your living space drains your energy, and what could shift that?

- Where are you waiting for permission to make a bold move in your home life?

Script Revision:

Every rehearsal ends with a new line to carry forward. Rewrite the script and let it guide your next decision:

"I create a home that reflects who I am and who I'm becoming. My space supports my peace, power, and possibility."

Encore: Home is a Place, a Feeling, and a Choice

Home isn't just where you live; it's where you become. It's the space that either drains your energy or fills your tank, depending on what you allow inside.

Your environment shapes everything: your nervous system, creativity, and sense of peace. When your space supports who you're becoming, you move through life grounded. When it doesn't, you start every day at a deficit. A healthy home is built through a series of bold choices: sometimes to stay, sometimes to leave, always to grow.

Improv taught me that we don't need perfect conditions to create something extraordinary. Performers build entire worlds on empty stages because they believe in what they're creating together. You can do the same. Every choice to declutter, redesign, or relocate becomes an act of self-respect and intention.

Your next chapter deserves a foundation that mirrors your growth, not your past. Start where you are. Adjust the scene. Make your space worthy of the life you're building.

The stage is yours. Step into it fully and make it a home.

Script Notes: Redefining Home on My Terms

These moments helped me reclaim the meaning of home on my terms, with my values, and without apology. Let them inspire your New Choice moments, where you stop waiting for permission and create a home life that feels like yours.

1. **Calling Out the Chaos**

My brother reached his breaking point and my mother's drinking could no longer be ignored, so I said the word out loud: alcoholic. His emotional outburst dismantled the family script of silence and taught me to trust my truth.

2. **Saying "Two Weeks" With Zero Plan**

Sitting at the dining room table, lit only by determination, I gave myself a deadline to move out of my parents' house. No savings. No blueprint. Just clarity. That declaration became my launchpad out of dysfunction.

3. **Buying Big When They Said Think Small**

I didn't want a starter condo. I wanted income, equity, and independence, so I bought a multi-unit building in my twenties, despite every "Are you sure?" from agents who underestimated me.

4. **Selling the Dream to Build a New One**

Letting go of my Chicago dream home wasn't a failure. I pivoted and used the sale to open a theater, naming it after the life I once thought I'd return to. My choice turned grief into creativity.

5. **Turning a Mobile Home into a Healing Space**

During my marital separation, I didn't wait for a dream house. I made the space I had feel like a haven of peace. That mobile home wasn't fancy, but it was mine, and it was enough.

6. **Drawing the Line Before the Foundation**

With my husband David, I refused to rent and "see what happens." We decided to build something real. The line in the sand marked the start of shared commitment, not shared compromise.

7. **Naming the Italy Dream Out Loud**

I want a home in Italy. The moment I said it out loud, it stopped being a fantasy and became a direction. Because naming the dream is how you start building toward it.

Chapter 8:
Choosing Family Roles

Redefining and Redesigning Family Dynamics

"Blood makes you related. Love and loyalty make you family."
— Katie Reus

Who You Choose Shapes Who You Become

People commonly say, "You can't choose your family." The phrase usually surfaces after holiday dinners featuring undercooked turkey, overcooked drama, and someone fake smiling through gritted teeth. While you cannot select your biological roots, you absolutely can choose who earns a seat at your table. Every invitation and boundary you set shapes your story and influences how you show up in the world.

I have made that choice repeatedly. Each decision brought unexpected resistance and freedom that felt like opening windows in rooms I hadn't realized were suffocating me.

Friends, coworkers, and chosen community often become the real family. They often show up with more love, loyalty, and fewer unsolicited opinions about your life choices. Research on chosen families highlights their decisive role in helping individuals heal from past relational trauma and develop healthier patterns of belonging (Weston, 1991). Potlucks improve dramatically when no one brings emotional baggage wrapped in foil.

The people around you do more than provide companionship. According to social learning theory, their habits, energy, and beliefs become part of your operating system, whether you consciously invite them in or not (Bandura, 1977). Their influence seeps into your daily choices, shaping how you think, act, and even feel about yourself.

Most people consult their inner circle when facing major decisions. Life rarely offers clarity in isolation. The voices you allow into your head matter, especially when they speak louder than your internal wisdom. Research confirms that emotionally supportive relationships increase our capacity for self-regulation, goal-setting, and decision-making (Epstein et al., 2012).

Supportive relationships create space for growth, while wrong ones keep you contracted and small. Your relational environment affects everything, either building you up or systematically wearing you down. Choose carefully.

The Science Behind the Family Albums

Before we ever learn to improvise, we learn to mimic. Family is our first stage. From the moment we enter the scene, we absorb lines, roles, and rhythms. Psychologist Albert Bandura referred to this as "social learning" where we observe, we imitate, we repeat (Bandura, 1977). Whether spoken or silently modeled, the behaviors we witness growing up shape our emotional instincts and decision-making defaults. Family systems theory goes even further: families don't just influence us, they script us. As Dr. Murray Bowen argued, we carry the emotional legacies of our families into every room we enter, often without even realizing it (Bowen, 1978). That explains why we might flinch at conflict, over-apologize, or chase approval like oxygen. We're not weak. We're rehearsed.

When those family dynamics are healthy, rooted in emotional safety, open communication, and mutual respect, they become a launchpad for resilience. Studies show that individuals raised in supportive family environments tend to make more confident life choices and build stronger relationships (Epstein et al., 2012). But when those environments are dysfunctional, the impact runs just as deep. Children adopt survival roles, such as the perfectionist hero or the invisible lost child, because these roles helped them survive. With awareness and support, we can rewrite those scripts. Healing begins with conscious, well-timed "new choices."

When Life Doesn't Go as Planned

Today, I am married for the second time and a stepmom. From a young age, I dreamed of being a wife and a mother. That dream took a few sharp turns.

There was the con artist you met in the finance chapter. There was my first husband, who stalled on marriage for years and eventually admitted he did not want children. Or maybe he just did not want them with me. By the time I saw that clearly, I was no longer in a place to have children biologically.

People always have suggestions. You can adopt, foster, or explore IVF. All of those are valid. I chose to keep moving forward and make the next right decision.

In time, I built a family that feels right, not just with my husband and stepson but also with his parents, who welcomed me in ways I never expected.

For years, I ached for the family I imagined. That longing pushed me to reflect, reinvent, and recalibrate. I asked myself what family really means to me. That question became my compass. It brought me here.

The Family I Came From

My mother struggled with alcoholism. My father's ties to organized crime created constant instability, even if I did not understand it at the time. Our home carried tension like a background hum. My dad treated me like royalty. My mom treated me like Cinderella. I bounced between feeling adored and discarded.

He placed me on a pedestal. That might sound like love, but it placed unrealistic expectations on me from a young age. Experts call it emotional abuse. I do not think he intended to hurt me, but the damage was done.

My younger brother had a different experience. He was my mother's clear favorite. Yes, parents have favorites. I will die on that hill. She and my brother moved in sync. My father and I had our bond. The house often felt divided into two teams.

Adding my father's first marriage made things even more complicated. I had two half-sisters. The oldest stayed close to him and played a pivotal role in my life. She was the one who told me to get out, go to college, and save myself. She saw what I couldn't. The other sister? I have never met her. She blamed our father for the divorce. Her view is valid, but it is not my story to tell.

When I got married for the first time, my one half-sister was the only one from my side who showed up. "Someone has to represent your family," she said. My mother didn't attend. Of all people, the wedding singer called it out. He asked, "Is your mother an alcoholic?" He said she probably skipped the wedding because she could not figure out how to hide her drinking. That was the moment I finally accepted my mother for who she was.

By then, my father had already passed. My brother walked me down the aisle. But the lines had already been drawn. After our dad died, my mother and brother became a united force and I was clearly on my own.

My mother and I spent years estranged. My brother often stood in the middle. He lived with her in a multi-unit property she bought. He paid very little, and their bond only deepened. I left the state and built a life with my first husband.

Loss, Betrayal, and the Will

In 2020, when COVID hit, my mom got sick. We were not speaking. When she entered hospice, my brother called. She wanted to see me.

I had always said that if she asked, I would go. No matter what. And I did.

I always showed up. Even when they abandoned me during the con artist nightmare, I came back. I wanted a connection. I missed my dad. I wanted to be the good daughter and the loyal sister.

After she passed, my brother and I planned the memorial together. She did not leave much. A little debt. A house. That house had initially been one of my dad's investments. I had once suggested putting it in a trust to protect it. That suggestion cost me more than I knew.

Before my mother passed, her attorney called and left me a voicemail by mistake. She thought she was speaking to my mother. "Are you sure you want to take your daughter out of the will?" she asked.

That was how I found out that my name had been removed from the trust.

I returned the attorney's call. She tried to walk the message back.

She said it wasn't true and that my mom told her she loved me. I chose not to press it because I knew it was my mother's disease trying to hurt me again.

Later, when it was time to settle the estate, everything came out. I had no legal right to the house. My brother never mentioned it. He reassured me and promised we would split things evenly.

Then, he asked me to co-sign a mortgage on a house I no longer had any claim to. When I said no, he turned on me and accused me of trying to take advantage of him.

Not long after, I received a cold email. "Do not contact me anymore. Communicate through my attorney."

The Moment Everything Shifted

I had just met David around that time. We had been seeing each other for two weeks when I shared the email with him.

His response was simple.

"You can let it go. I'm your family now."

Hearing those words stirred up more than I expected. Part of me felt comforted. Part of me felt skeptical. We had just met. I chose to believe him anyway.

Two weeks later, I joined him and his son on a road trip to visit his parents in the mountains of Pennsylvania. Fourteen hours in a car with a teenager will reveal everything. When we arrived, David's parents welcomed me without hesitation. They treated me like I belonged.

In that moment, I felt something I had not felt in decades. I felt at home.

I Chose Myself

What brought me to that moment was choice. I chose to walk away from my biological family. I decided to stop chasing people who never made space for me. Therapy helped me see how much of my pain was rooted in my relationship with my mother. I stopped needing her love to define me.

When she died, I felt peace. Then I felt guilty. I told my therapist I was worried that I was not grieving. She reminded me that I grieved my mother's death in therapy. That conversation gave me the permission I needed to move forward.

Walking away from my brother was harder. He was the last connection to my childhood. In the past, I would have fought to stay close. I believed in loyalty, redemption, and the idea that family is forever.

Then David repeated it.

"Let it go. I'm your family now."

That was the moment I broke the cycle. That was my new choice. I chose to stop doing the same thing and expecting something different. I still believe in forgiveness. I always will. Forgiveness allowed me to walk away without hate. I can forgive my brother. I do. But I will not forget. I do not have to go back.

Breaking the Cycle

Patterns are meant to be broken. Change begins when you stop performing the same scene out of habit.

I used a clear framework to shift old dynamics and show up differently. Each move helped me respond with more intention, less reactivity, and a stronger sense of self.

You can apply the same patterns. Practice them. Let them guide your next choice:

- Introduce contrast. Respond to hostility with clarity. Choose calm instead of chaos. Choose silence instead of escalation.

- Disrupt default roles. Stop replaying the character others expect. Make a new move. Choose a new direction.

- Practice presence. Show up fully. You are not who you were. This moment is yours.

How Improv Helped Me with Family Dynamics

Before stepping onto an improv stage, I was already deep in the most unscripted performance of my life: navigating family dynamics. No script. No rehearsal. Just a lot of emotion, expectation, and the urge to either fix everything or flee the scene. I didn't realize it at the time, but I was stuck in a role I hadn't auditioned for, feeling reactive, defensive, and often exhausted. Improv snuck in, not as a performance trick, but as a life tool. A new language that allowed me, and the practice I needed, to rewrite how I showed up in those roles. Especially the ones that hit closest to home.

Improv snuck in not as a performance trick, but as a life tool. What I love about improv is that we don't need to stay in character. Therapists use improv for this very reason because it allows people to safely disrupt old roles and explore new ways of relating, especially within families (Phillips, 2021).

 Communication changed first. I stopped rushing to fix and started listening more deeply. Improv taught me the value of silence; not passive silence but the kind that creates space. Making that shift alone transformed how I connected with people I used to clash with. Listening without filling the space changed everything.

Adaptability came next. Families don't stay the same. Roles evolve. Relationships shift. Improv helped me stop clinging to old identities. I no longer tried to control the storyline. I learned how to meet change with presence and curiosity. When I became a stepmom, no book could prepare me. Improv gave me one golden rule: follow the follower. I let my stepson lead. Our connection grew from there.

Collaboration replaced control. Once I stopped trying to have all the answers, our family began to co-create solutions. We moved from competing preferences to shared decisions. Even planning a trip became a team effort. Improv showed me how to build with others instead of trying to lead every scene.

Disruption became a tool, not a trigger. I didn't have to match defensiveness. Instead, I could flex my style with playfulness, surprise, or silence. Contrast, an improv technique, became my ally, reshaping how I engaged with old patterns without confrontation or drama.

Research supports this. Improv helps families actively listen, build empathy, and rewrite unhelpful patterns (Phillips, 2021; Second City, 2023). Flexibility, emotional safety, and connection all emerge from this practice, creating the essential ingredients for a healthier family system.

Improv allowed me to choose a new way to show up, not just on stage but at home, in relationships, and every moment. When the roles others gave me no longer fit, I rewrote the scene.

You Get to Choose

Family stories can be messy. Complicated. Painful. But no matter where yours began, you have choices now.

Many people sacrifice their health, happiness, and identity just to be seen as "good." They disappear, trying to meet expectations rooted in dysfunction.

No one deserves your loyalty more than you.

Choosing yourself is not selfish. Sometimes it is the only way to become the version of yourself you were meant to be.

You cannot be a good family member while being treated like you don't matter.

The story you inherited does not have to be the one you continue. Family can mean alignment. Shared values. Emotional safety.

I used to believe love meant tolerating mistreatment. Now, I believe love is built on respect, and that begins with how you treat yourself.

How to Choose Your Own Family Dynamics & Legacy

You can't rewrite the past. You can reshape what comes next. Here's how to start:

Scene Work:

Take the stage and move from theory to practice with these quick drills to help you catch your defaults, pivot in the moment, and train your brain for change.

- Identify and Rewrite Family Rules: Name three unspoken family rules you absorbed growing up. Ask if they still serve you. Rewrite one rule to align with who you are now.

- Choose One Relationship to Approach Differently: Select one family relationship where you want to try a new dynamic. Practice setting one boundary or having one honest conversation.

- Define Your Chosen Family: List people who genuinely support your growth, whether related by blood or not. Consider how you can strengthen these relationships.

Side Coaching

Before making more choices, pause and check in. The following prompts will help you be honest about what's on autopilot and what needs to change.

- Where are you still reenacting old family roles that no longer fit?

- Where are you finally ready to say no to unhealthy patterns?

- What does "chosen family" mean to you now?

Script Revision:

Every rehearsal ends with a new line to carry forward. Rewrite the script and let it guide your next decision:

"I honor where I come from and choose relationships that help me grow forward."

Encore: Build the Family That Feels Like Home

Choosing your family is a series of conscious decisions about who influences your story. Sociologist Kath Weston (1991) coined the term *"families we choose"* to describe these chosen kinships that provide the acceptance and security our birth families sometimes can't. Every day, you decide which voices to amplify, which relationships to nurture, and which patterns to break or continue.

The family you were born into provided your origin story, not your destiny. The early chapters of your life may have taught you some beautiful and painful lessons, but they don't dictate how your story ends. You hold the pen now.

Real family shows up consistently. They celebrate your growth instead of trying to contain it. They offer love without conditions, support without strings attached. Sometimes that family shares your DNA. Sometimes they're the people who choose you back when you choose them.

Building a chosen family requires courage. Walking away from dysfunction, even when it wears the mask of loyalty, takes strength. Setting boundaries with blood relatives who drain your energy is a form of self-preservation, not betrayal. Saying yes to relationships that nourish you isn't selfish.

Your story doesn't end with the wounds you inherited. Healing occurs when you stop waiting for damaged people to become whole and start surrounding yourself with those who are already doing their own work. Peace comes when you release the fantasy of who people could be and embrace the reality of who they are.

The most profound act of love you can offer is showing up authentically in relationships that welcome your whole self. When you stop performing roles that never fit, you create space for genuine connection to flourish.

You weren't meant to shrink to make others comfortable. You weren't designed to carry everyone else's emotional baggage. You deserve relationships that grow you, not relationships that diminish you.

Your next chapter begins with one bold decision: to choose relationships that nourish your growth. Psychologists refer to this as the intergenerational challenge, recognizing that cycles of dysfunction are not predetermined, and that healing begins with conscious, new choices (Psych Central, 2023; King University Online, 2017).

Choose the people who see your potential and cheer for your success. Choose the family that feels like home, that creates safety instead of chaos, and that builds you up instead of wearing you down.

Script Notes: Redefining Family on My Terms

These moments helped me break free from patterns, set boundaries, and redefine what family means on my terms. Use them as inspiration to spot your New Choice moments, where you stop repeating the old script and start writing something new.

1. Saying Yes to College, Not Chaos

I listened when my oldest half-sister told me to leave and save myself. I chose education over entanglement. That decision planted the first seed of independence and set me on the path toward the life I wanted, not the one I inherited.

2. Showing Up in Hospice After Estrangement

When my mother was dying, she asked to see me. I went. That choice was not about her redemption. It was about mine.

3. Refusing to Co-Sign the Mortgage

After learning I had been removed from the trust, my brother asked me to co-sign a loan. I said no. That marked the shift from appeasement to self-respect.

4. Allowing a New Definition of Family

Two weeks into dating David, he said, "I'm your family now." I let the words land. I chose to believe in the possibility of new love, loyalty, and belonging.

5. Letting Go of the Title "Daughter" and "Sister"

I stopped trying to earn love from people who treated me as if I were expendable. Letting go of the fantasy that biology equals bond gave me the freedom to write a new story.

6. Choosing Forgiveness Without Reconciliation

Forgiveness does not require reunion. I forgave my mother and my brother. I did not re-enter the cycle. That choice made space for healing without reopening old wounds.

7. Embracing My Role as Stepmom

Becoming a stepmom was not my imagined path, but I leaned in with an open heart. I poured into the family that chose me, building trust one small moment at a time.

Chapter 9
Choosing Love That Grows

Rewriting Relationship Patterns with Clarity

"The best love is the kind that awakens the soul and makes us reach for more. It plants a fire in our hearts and brings peace to our minds." — Nicholas Sparks

According to a 2021 study published in Interpersona, relationship satisfaction accounts for up to 21 percent of a person's overall life satisfaction. A statistic like this makes sense to me, as I am a forever hopeless romantic who thrives in every aspect of life with the right partner. Love isn't a side dish. Love is a central ingredient in well-being, happiness, and a sense of purpose.

I've long been in love with the idea of love itself. For as long as I can remember, having a true partner who can be my best friend, family, and intimate match is a dream and the foundation for "la dolce vita" – the sweet life.

Being boy crazy at a young age, my first crush was in kindergarten. His name was David, and he asked me to marry him. I've never written about this before, and as I type it now, I'm struck by the fact that I eventually did marry David. Just not the first David I met. Serendipity? Maybe.

One moment sparked a lifelong desire to share love deeply, fully, and with intention.

My parents' marriage broke convention, but it proved that enduring love could still thrive. Their bond showed me that even imperfect relationships can be deeply meaningful, and that genuine connection is possible. They were playful and silly together. My father always kissed her hello and goodbye when leaving and returning home. I knew I wanted that kind of marriage. Everyone assumed I would be the first in my friend group to get married and have children. Instead, I became the last to walk down the aisle, the first time, at 43. I never imagined I'd also be the one without biological children.

The phrase 'unlucky in love' always made me cringe, yet it felt true for a long time. Through therapy and hard-earned healing, I discovered the real story. Before I could love anyone else, I had to learn how to love myself. That meant untangling childhood trauma, rewriting my worth, and choosing growth over repetition.

Dating in today's world adds another layer: Swiping, ghosting, and emotional unavailability. Finding someone compatible is hard enough, let alone someone healed, honest, and ready. In a swipe-happy, instant-gratification culture, many people feel hopeless about love.

Ironically, I met my husband on Tinder, a dating app. Swiping right led me to true love. That swipe was only the start. The real path required intention, resilience, and a willingness to improvise. I kissed a lot of frogs. I stayed curious. I rewrote my script again and again, making new choices until the right one stuck.

Choosing Love: The Improv of My Life

Starting over in my 50s wasn't part of any master plan. After ending an emotionally abusive marriage, I felt simultaneously exhausted and energized. Years of therapy clarified what I deserved, and I finally possessed the courage to claim it.

My first marriage had left me financially and emotionally depleted. No savings account, detailed roadmap, or elaborate backup plan; just a temporary rental property, a laptop, and unshakeable conviction that I would prioritize my wellbeing this time.

Writing a new dating profile felt like drawing a line in the sand. The message was direct: "Have your shit together. Be genuinely happy with yourself. Be emotionally strong enough to love a confident woman who doesn't need rescuing but still wants partnership."

Writing a bold profile required the same courage as stepping onto an improv stage, showing up authentically without knowing how the scene would end. In Dare to Lead, Brené Brown's research on vulnerability, shame, and wholehearted living reframed my understanding of courage. She writes that vulnerability is not the opposite of strength but rather its foundation: the willingness to show up when there are no guarantees. That insight echoed what improvisation had already taught me: the most powerful performances, and the most meaningful relationships, begin when we stop trying to control the outcome and simply respond truthfully in the moment. Both improv and Brown's work challenged the same lifelong instinct I had to perform for approval. They called me to let go of the polished version of myself and practice something scarier: being seen exactly as I am.

Both demanded I stop performing and start being real.

Two days later, David (my now husband) messaged me for the first time.

He suggested dinner. Actual dinner, not just casual drinks. We went to my favorite quiet restaurant, tucked away from the usual crowds. Mid-conversation, he asked if I liked banana bread. I said yes. At evening's end, he asked permission to kiss me. I said yes again. Then he handed me a homemade loaf of banana bread for my upcoming business trip.

Kindness radiated from him. Intelligence, emotional maturity, and humor came naturally. Most remarkably, he felt familiar, like coming home to myself.

Months later, I discovered the list I had created in therapy, the detailed description of qualities I truly wanted in a partner. When I shared it with David, he laughed and asked, "Did you write this about me?" My answer: "Yes, I did, years before we ever met."

One year later, I married him.

David doesn't complete me; he complements me. Therapy restored my sense of worth. David created space for me to receive love without diminishing myself.

If you're feeling trapped, afraid to leave, or convinced it's too late to find love that feels like a sanctuary, let me be clear: you're wrong.

Love operates like improvisation. The most beautiful scenes emerge when you gather enough courage to declare, "This isn't workng. I'm ready to create something entirely new."

The Facts About Love

Love isn't reserved for fairytales or the fortunate few. Connection represents a fundamental human need backed by decades of research. Satisfying relationships correlate with greater life satisfaction, enhanced emotional regulation, improved physical health, and increased longevity. Quality partnerships reduce cortisol levels, lower blood pressure, decrease inflammation, and strengthen immune function. Love doesn't just feel good; it literally heals your body.

Friendship: The Foundation of Lasting Love

Enduring romantic relationships often grow from solid foundations of friendship. Strong couples prioritize emotional intimacy through consistent trust-building, aligned values, and genuine connection. Research from Utah State University suggests that friendship within marriage fosters resilience, joy, and emotional safety. This security becomes the fertile ground where more profound love can flourish.

Meeting David didn't immediately spark romantic certainty. One truth emerged clearly: friendship had to establish itself first. That bond became our intimacy, our stability, and our quiet superpower, carrying us through every challenge.

Self-Love and Healing: The Prerequisites to Healthy Partnership

Personal healing work cannot be bypassed or rushed. Self-awareness and emotional health have a direct impact on relationship quality. Unaddressed trauma distorts connection patterns, causing people to repeat destructive cycles. Emotional unavailability becomes familiar. Chaos masquerades as chemistry. Drama feels like passion.

Therapy exposed the harmful scripts that had shaped my relationship choices for decades. Resources like the book *Attached* provided language for patterns I had unconsciously repeated. Recognition created the possibility for genuine change.

Recovery happens incrementally, scene by scene. Growth gradually reshapes your story until trauma no longer controls the narrative.

The Role of Serendipity: Love Isn't Always Logical

Perfect preparation cannot guarantee ideal timing. Love appears unexpectedly through dating apps, after profound loss, or during quiet moments of surrender. Research on synchronicity suggests that openness to uncertainty often precedes life-changing encounters.

David and I had likely crossed paths multiple times before our official meeting. Previous timing hadn't been appropriately aligned. Then one pivotal moment shifted everything.

Some love stories defy logic and planning. The best ones often do.

Why Love Transforms Everything

Authentic love creates space for complete transformation. True partnership provides room to grow, fail, recover, and evolve without fear of abandonment.

Relationships built on self-awareness, rooted in genuine friendship, and open to life's beautiful surprises offer one of existence's most profound adventures. Love doesn't complete you; it reveals who you were always meant to become.

The Science of Choosing Connection

Love is more than romantic sentiment or wishful thinking; it is measurable medicine for human well-being. Decades of research demonstrate that emotionally supportive relationships rank among the most potent predictors of overall life satisfaction, physical health, and longevity.

Quality connections reduce cortisol production, strengthen immune function, lower the risk of cardiovascular disease, and can potentially extend lifespan by up to seven years.

A comprehensive 2021 longitudinal study revealed that relationship satisfaction directly accounts for up to 21 percent of individual life satisfaction scores. Simply put: the quality of your romantic relationship measurably determines how satisfied you feel with your entire life.

Genuine connection transcends initial chemistry or physical attraction. Lasting bonds develop through trust-building, emotional safety, nervous system co-regulation, and mutual commitment to growth. Each element strengthens through the accumulation of daily choices: how deeply we listen, how thoughtfully we respond, and how skillfully we repair inevitable ruptures.

Improvisation cultivates these exact relational skills. "Yes, And" transforms from performance technique into connection methodology. Regular practice develops validation abilities, present-moment awareness, and forward momentum even when outcomes remain uncertain or uncomfortable.

Neuroscience reveals that healthy relationships literally rewire our brains for resilience. Secure attachment patterns can develop at any age through consistent, responsive interactions. Mirror neurons activate when partners demonstrate empathy, creating biological synchronization that deepens emotional bonds.

Love flourishes through conscious choice rather than circumstance, luck, or effortless compatibility. Successful relationships require deliberate cultivation, emotional intelligence, and commitment to authentically showing up during harmony and conflict.

The most resilient partnerships begin with one fundamental decision: to remain emotionally engaged regardless of temporary difficulties.

Scene by scene, conversation by conversation, choice by choice, love becomes a practiced art form rather than a fleeting feeling.

What's Improv Got to Do With It?

Authentic love operates without predetermined scripts. Each meaningful moment emerges through genuine co-creation between partners. Improvisation taught me essential relationship skills: deep listening, emotional risk-taking, and showing up authentically in every interaction.

Love, like improvisation, demands complete presence. Generosity of spirit becomes essential. Curiosity fuels growth and connection. Questions like "If this, then what?" propel relationships forward through inevitable challenges.

The improv exercise "New Choice" transformed my entire dating approach. Each time something failed or felt misaligned, I made deliberate pivots. I chose differently, consciously, courageously.

Before discovering improv, I approached dating like a prolonged audition. Performance felt to be necessary to earn love and acceptance.

Experience taught me otherwise.

Improvisation revealed that genuine connection emerges from being fully present, listening without an agenda, and showing up without rehearsed personas.

When I abandoned the script, authentic love finally had space to enter.

The "Yes, And" Choice

"Yes, And" originated as an improvisation technique but evolved into my primary love language and communication framework.

"Yes, I hear your perspective completely. And here's what I need as well."

Validation combined with contribution creates forward momentum. During conflicts, this approach generates safety and understanding. In moments of connection, it deepens intimacy and mutual respect.

Choosing Vulnerability

Love requires profound emotional risk. Authentic exposure becomes the necessary cost of genuine connection. Truth must consistently supersede comfort. Courage leads every meaningful conversation.

Improvisation provided a safe practice space for radical honesty. There were no scripts, just presence, authentic response, and mutual trust. Awkward silences, uncertain beginnings, and unexpected turns became tools for building resilience. Each moment presented a choice to remain emotionally open.

Vulnerability appears in every relationship-defining moment. Speaking brutal truths matters more than maintaining temporary harmony. Asking challenging questions matters more than preserving surface-level peace. Choosing to stay engaged or choosing to leave reveals the deepest expressions of genuine care.

Some stories naturally complete their arc. Releasing what no longer serves can honor love more deeply than desperate clinging. Strength manifests through the graceful acceptance of what no longer fits.

Improvisation trained essential emotional muscles for all of these challenges: failing gracefully, finding humor in difficulty, resetting after conflict, and returning to connection. Each scene offered another opportunity to choose authenticity over performance. Love deserves nothing less than complete honesty.

Keeping Love Alive Through Play

One of improvisation's most valuable relationship lessons is that joy remains a continuous choice, not a one-time discovery.

Many people treat love like a destination rather than a journey. Finding someone becomes the goal, followed by emotional autopilot. Love, like improvisation, cannot thrive without conscious engagement. Growth requires both partners to consistently demonstrate responsibility, commitment, creativity, curiosity, and playfulness.

Improvisation teaches you to follow delight and energy. Rather than forcing what isn't working, you pivot toward possibility. Fresh offers get made. Surprise becomes integral to the process.

Healthy relationships benefit from this same adaptive spirit. Play prevents stagnation. Lightness enters when heaviness threatens to overwhelm. Even during difficult seasons, joy remains accessible.

When relationships feel disconnected, monotonous, or overly serious, play restores vitality. Moods shift naturally. Hearts reopen. Both partners receive permission to embrace their full humanity. Laughter, experimentation, and graceful mistakes are all hallmarks of improvisational thinking that help couples reconnect throughout their journey.

Play deserves recognition as foundational rather than frivolous. Research consistently shows that couples prioritizing shared fun and laughter experience greater satisfaction and resilience.

Communication flows more naturally and honestly. Tension becomes manageable without emotional shutdown. Shared activities create a common language for navigating conflict while building mutual joy that sustains daily life.

Improvisation provided the framework. Building together, even during disagreement, became possible. Changing direction without shame became natural. Curiosity remained alive years into the relationship. Personal growth accelerates rather than ending when love begins.

Exercises For Choosing Love, Your Way

The following exercises will help you improvise love with intention, whether you're healing, dating, or deepening a connection. Think of them as your personal rehearsal space for love that's present, playful, and real.

Scene Work:

Take the stage and move from theory to practice with these quick drills to help you catch your defaults, pivot in the moment, and train your brain for change.

- New Choice Dating Reframe Journal: "What story have I been telling myself about love, and how is it keeping me stuck?" Use "New Choice" to rewrite limiting beliefs about relationships.

- Practice "Yes, And" in Conflict: Consider a recent disagreement. Practice responding: "Yes, I hear you're feeling _____. And I want to understand better so we can figure this out together."

- Relationship Vision Improvisation: Revisit your ideal partner list. Add: "What's one unexpected quality that would delight me?" and "What's one thing I didn't originally include that now feels essential?"

Side Coaching:

Before making more choices, pause and check in. The following prompts will help you be honest about what's on autopilot and what needs to change.

- What old story about love has shaped your choices, and how might it be limiting you?
- What does emotional safety feel like, and when did you last experience it?
- What kind of relationship would your healthiest self create, and how are you prepared to show up differently?

Script Revision:

Every rehearsal ends with a new line to carry forward. Rewrite the script and let it guide your next decision:

> *"I choose love that honors who I am, not who I pretend to be. I am worthy of connection that meets me in truth and grows with me in trust."*

Encore: Rewriting The Love Story

Love doesn't follow a script. Authentic connection requires presence, courage, and the willingness to choose growth over comfort.

Improvisation teaches essential relationship skills, including listening deeply, speaking truthfully, and reconnecting after conflict. "Yes, And" becomes a love language. "New Choice" becomes a dating philosophy. Vulnerability transforms from risk into strength.

The most profound relationships don't complete you; they reveal who you were always meant to become. They create space for your authentic self while accepting your full humanity.

Love rewards those brave enough to show up consistently and imperfectly. Stop waiting for perfect conditions. Stop performing for approval.

Your next chapter begins with one decision: to choose connection over protection, authenticity over performance.

Show up as you are. Choose again when things get difficult. Love finds those willing to receive it without masks or pretenses.

The stage is set. Make it worthy of the love you've always deserved.

Script Notes: How I Improvised My Way to Love

These are the new choices that shaped my journey to finding healthy, lasting love. Use them as inspiration to script your own.

1. **Writing a Bold Dating Profile**

After years of trying to sound "palatable," I finally wrote what I really meant: *"Have your shit together."* That choice cut through the noise and attracted someone who could meet me where I was - confident, clear, and ready.

2. **Going on the "Costa" Date Anyway**

Part of me wanted to cancel. I was tired, skeptical, and jaded. I went anyway. The choice to meet David led me to banana bread, a real kiss, and the love of my life.

3. **Choosing to Stay Curious, Not Cynical**

I could have written David off as "too good to be true." Instead, I stayed open. Making that choice made space for something real to unfold.

4. **Saying No to Settling (Again)**

Leaving my first marriage was a reclamation and a choice to reset my standard: I would never again beg to be chosen. I would pick myself first.

5. **Dating with Intention, Not Desperation**

I didn't wait for love to find me. I dated with clarity, practiced resilience, and kissed a lot of frogs, a choice that made finding my king possible.

6. **Letting the List Lead Me**

The list I made in therapy became my guide and a choice that kept me grounded when charm threatened to cloud my vision.

7. **Choosing Love Without Losing Myself**

David complemented me. The choice to seek someone who complemented my wholeness changed every aspect of my life.

Chapter 10
Choosing The Right Circle of Friends

Casting the Right People for the Life You're Leading

"True friends are families which you can select."
— Audrey Hepburn

Your friends, your network, your community. These relationships shape how you live, lead, and show up. The line between personal and professional often blurs, but the impact stays real.

Friendship carries as much influence as family. In some seasons, even more.

Connection surrounds us, but authenticity feels harder to find. Social media shows us faces, but few of those people would answer a midnight call.

Every voice in your circle affects how you think, how you heal, and how far you grow. Choosing those voices with intention is an act of self-respect.

The Definition of Friendship

I've sat through leadership trainings where consultants preach the importance of having a life beyond work. Yet many high achievers hit retirement with no real hobbies, no meaningful community, and no idea who they are without a job title. Their entire identity lived inside their career. Then it ended.

Social media only makes things worse. The word "friend" has lost its weight. My feed is full of names, but few represent real support.

For years, I believed I had a strong network. On paper, it looked impressive: thousands of contacts, a high follower count. But my real support system? That list was short. When life fell apart, only a handful of people showed up. The rest were just noise.

True friends don't flinch when things get messy. They ask hard questions when needed, but they lead with support. They listen. They challenge. They make room. And they show up without asking for a performance.

The best ones live out the "Yes, and" principle of improv. They accept without judgment, then help you build from there.

The Network Theory

During a psychology of leadership course, I studied how relationships affect performance. The takeaway was clear: every person in your circle either helps or hinders your momentum.

Most people fall into one of three categories:

- Supporters: They believe in your potential and lift you up.

- Detractors: They smile on the surface but quietly root against your growth.

- Neutrals: They stay in your orbit but add no real energy.

While teaching this framework to a client, she flipped the script and introduced a fourth category I've used ever since.

- Challengers: People who know you well enough to push you. They ask hard questions and disrupt your comfort zone in service of your growth.

That client taught me something I hadn't seen for myself. In that moment, I got to practice what I preach. I made a new choice.

That insight reshaped how I viewed my circle. Plenty of people I had called friends didn't earn that title. Once I saw their roles clearly, I stopped assigning top billing to people who belonged offstage.

When "Friends" Become Detractors

That framework became personal during a major shift in my life. I had committed to a health journey. I lost 80 pounds, stopped drinking, and focused on rebuilding from the inside out.

Someone I once considered a best friend reacted with frustration. She missed the wine nights, and her disappointment unsettled me. She knew I was trying to save my first marriage, and she knew what I was fighting for.

When I asked for support, she offered silence. That told me more than words ever could.

Later, during the divorce, the pattern repeated. People disappeared. Some had been in my life long before I met my first husband. They claimed neutrality, but their absence spoke volumes.

Divorce reveals who stands with you. Many say they will not take sides. Their silence often does it for them.

Those losses hurt, but they also cleared space for people who could meet me where I was going, not where I had been.

The Friendship That Taught Me to Say "New Choice"

One friendship exposed a destructive pattern I had been repeating for years. The revelation came gradually through accumulated moments rather than sudden dramatic confrontation, building toward an inevitable and necessary shift.

Michelle started as a coaching client and evolved into a friend. Her life operated on perpetual chaos: failed marriages, parenting struggles, and career confusion. I recognized her as a fellow survivor. I had navigated my version of that turbulence.

During my first marriage breakdown, she issued a blunt warning. Staying in the relationship would destroy my business. I needed therapy immediately. Her tone felt condescending. She perceived me as someone unraveling. I viewed myself as maintaining control through pain, as someone skilled at performing stability.

Her words stung but propelled me forward. I pursued therapy and created an exit plan. Her delivery lacked compassion, but the outcome brought essential clarity.

Years later, Michelle remained trapped in familiar patterns. A new marriage provided surface stability, but direction still eluded her. I introduced her to women in my client circle, hoping she might find belonging. Female friendships had constantly challenged her, something she readily acknowledged.

Everything shattered during one group session. Michelle publicly challenged my guidance, not with genuine curiosity or constructive criticism, but with hostility. These weren't just friends present; they were paying clients who had trusted me. She created a scene that damaged the credibility I had spent years building.

The moment wasn't the first warning sign. However, it became the final one.

I waited for an apology that never materialized. She removed herself from the group and disappeared without explanation.

Months later, she left a voicemail claiming confusion about my anger. Her lack of awareness revealed everything about our dynamic. Authentic friendship requires mutual understanding and accountability.

Michelle had never earned a place in my inner circle during life's most difficult seasons. Real friends occupied that sacred space: people who showed up consistently, offered support without conditions, and cared without hidden agendas or personal gain.

After her departure, escalation followed. She contacted my workplace, jeopardizing my employment. She mailed anonymous, typed letters quoting obscure musical lyrics. I returned one with a single word: "Delusional."

My husband, a police officer, advised filing a restraining order if she made further contact. Fortunately, she never did.

The Science of Connection: Why We Need Friends

Human connection begins early and runs deep. Our brains are wired for friendship. Research shows that social bonding activates the brain's reward system, syncing emotional responses with those we trust. When a close friend feels joy or pain, the brain responds as if the experience is ours. That kind of empathy is both emotional and biological.

These bonds once helped our ancestors survive. Today, they still shape how we cope, grow, and thrive. Friendship is about resilience, not about convenience. As we get older, forming those connections takes more intention. Childhood teaches us how to bond. Adulthood teaches us how to choose.

The Neuroscience of Better Friendship

Friendship activates mirror neurons, aligning your emotional state with someone else's. That is why connection feels so rewarding. Practicing improv builds on this natural wiring while strengthening the neural pathways that support emotional awareness, quick adaptation, and relational recovery.

Improv sharpens the skills that matter most in friendship, specifically reading the room, showing up fully, and responding with care. The more we practice, the more those patterns become second nature. Improv helps you connect more honestly. Neuroscience explains why it works.

How Improv Strengthens Friendships

Improvisation changed the way I navigate friendship. The science behind it explains why it makes sense. Practicing improv strengthens the neural pathways responsible for healthy connection, empathy, and trust. Applying improv skills also helps us show up with authenticity and read the room while we're at it.

Repeated practice created a clear shift in how I listened, responded, and stayed present.

One of my improv teachers gave me the best advice in my first year of training. He said, "Never lose your childlike sense of wonder." The phrase stuck. Wonder invites vulnerability.

Vulnerability deepens connection. Science confirms the power of authenticity. Genuine expression activates the brain's reward system. When people feel safe to be real, trust grows. Trust builds strong friendships.

Improvisation rewired old habits. Control is used to lead many conversations. The urge to steer or fix often took over. "Yes, And" introduced a new rhythm. Collaboration replaced control.

Mutual respect followed. Partnership began to feel natural.

Friendships moved across different circles. Staying in one lane never felt right. Fluidity opened space for deeper bonds with people from all backgrounds. Improv strengthened that ability.

Practice trained my mind to welcome unfamiliar perspectives without losing personal grounding.

Reading the room became second nature. A missed beat, a pause, a shift in tone. Each cue helped shape my response. Boundaries became easier to honor. Respect followed presence. Conflict surfaced, as it does in any close connection.

Scene work prepared me to respond calmly. There was no need to defend or overpower. Listening with patience softened tense moments. Empathy guided the conversation. Trust deepened.

Casting Call: Who Belongs on The Stage Of Life With You?

"You become like the five people you spend the most time with. Choose carefully." — Jim Rohn

Now it's your turn to direct your cast.

Every relationship plays a role in the story of your life. Some people deserve a leading role. Others may belong in the background, or off the stage entirely. Choosing your friends is an act of self-respect and self-direction.

Scene Work:

Take the stage and move from theory to practice with these quick drills to help you catch your defaults, pivot in the moment, and train your brain for change.

- Cast Your Community: List the people who dominate your emotional, professional, or social space. Categorize each as a Supporter, Detractor, Neutral, or Challenger.

- Check the Chemistry: After casting your community, ask yourself, "How do I feel after spending time with them: energized, neutral, or drained?" and "Can I be my authentic self with them?"

- Make One Casting Change: Choose one relationship where something needs to shift. Be open to setting boundaries, changing the dynamic, or limiting someone's influence.

Side Coaching:

Before making more choices, pause and check in. The following prompts will help you be honest about what's on autopilot and what needs to change.

- Who's taking up space in your life who doesn't belong in a starring role?

- Who deserves more time and energy from you?

- What boundary would help you move someone from an "inner circle" to a "supportive background"?

Script Revision:

Every rehearsal ends with a new line to carry forward. Try this one on and let it guide your next decision:

> *"I am the director of my life and cast people who challenge me to grow, not people who ask me to shrink."*

Encore: Closing the Curtain, Opening the Door

Friendship isn't about collecting contacts or maintaining appearances. Real connection requires intentional choices about who has access to your energy, dreams, and most vulnerable moments.

Improvisation can help you recognize when a scene no longer serves the story. The same principle applies to relationships. Some friendships need clear endings, and others require boundaries. The healthiest ones grow alongside your evolution.

Your circle shapes everything: how you think, how you heal, how far you stretch toward your potential. Supporters lift you. Challengers push you forward. Detractors drain your momentum. Neutrals take up space without adding value.

Choose supporters who believe in your growth. Embrace challengers who ask hard questions from a place of love. Release detractors who smile while secretly hoping you fail. Limit neutrals who consume energy without contributing meaning.

My good friend Bob Burg reminds us in *The Go-Giver* that those who gain the most are the ones who give without keeping score. His philosophy helped me redefine success and friendship at the same time. True allies don't measure reciprocity in transactions; they measure it in trust. The people who became my strongest supporters showed up consistently, offered help without expectation, and celebrated my wins without jealousy or comparison. Their generosity wasn't performative; it was a reflection of abundance. They understood that giving freely doesn't diminish your worth; it multiplies it. That mindset became the foundation of every relationship I now choose to keep close.

Quality matters more than quantity. A small, sacred circle of authentic connections carries more power than hundreds of superficial relationships. The right people expand your vision and let you breathe fully. The wrong ones ask you to shrink.

Stop performing for friendship. Stop begging for a place in someone else's story. Start casting people who show up with truth, care, and genuine reciprocity.

Some relationships run their natural course, while others transform through mutual growth. Wisdom lies in recognizing the difference and responding with courage.

Your life deserves a supporting cast that champions your highest self. Not everyone earns a leading role. Choose the voices that expand your possibilities rather than limit them.

The stage is yours to direct. Cast wisely.

Script Notes: Redefining Friendship on My Terms

These are the bold choices that redefined my friendships. Use them as fuel to spark your new choice moments.

1. Walking Away from Michelle

When her behavior crossed a line in front of my clients, I didn't explain, excuse, or end it. My new choice broke a pattern of tolerating toxicity in the name of loyalty.

2. Saying No to Wine Nights

I chose my health. I stopped drinking. A friend took it personally. I let her reaction reveal the limits of the relationship. My new choice showed me who could support growth and who couldn't.

3. Allowing Distance to Become Clarity

Some friendships faded during hard seasons. I used to chase those people. Now I let the silence speak. My new choice created space for a genuine connection to take root.

4. Letting a Friend Come Back

One friendship was rekindled years after it had ended. We both needed time to grow. We reconnected, not from nostalgia, but from truth. My new choice honored the person I had become and the work we had both done.

5. Choosing Fewer, Deeper Connections

I used to collect people; Now, I curate. My new choice trimmed the noise and amplified the trust.

6. Showing Up as Myself, Not a Performer

Friendship used to feel like a role I had to earn. Now I choose people who see the real me and stick around anyway.

Chapter 11

Choosing To Grow

The Decision to Progress

"You walk in with so much confidence. But you don't have self-worth." — Liz Prete (Gina's therapist)

What Does Personal Growth Really Mean?

Personal development isn't a luxury for people with spare time and perfect lives. Growth becomes essential when your current way of operating stops working, old patterns create new problems, and you realize that who you've been isn't who you need to become.

Most people wait for the right moment to invest in themselves. The promotion, the empty nest, the perfect work-life balance. Meanwhile, life keeps accelerating, demands keep multiplying, and mythical "someday" never arrives.

Recent research spotlights a widening gap between the desire for personal development and the ability to act on it. According to Harvard Business Review Analytic Services, 70% of leaders acknowledge the importance of self-development, yet many struggle to find the time, resources, or support to pursue it meaningfully. Even more telling, 30 to 50% of leaders don't actively prioritize personal growth, despite knowing how critical it is to their success and fulfillment.

Organizational support isn't much better. According to the Center for Creative Leadership, only 34% of leaders report having access to formal leadership development programs, leaving many to navigate their growth alone.

The gap between knowing and doing explains why many people feel stuck, overwhelmed, or disconnected from their potential. Knowledge without action creates frustration. Awareness without change breeds resentment. Waiting to grow until things slow down usually means you never will. Life doesn't slow down until it comes to an end.

Personal growth has never followed a straight line or a prescribed formula. Growth has looked like therapy sessions that cracked me open, coaching conversations that shifted my perspective, failures that became my most outstanding teachers, and honest reflection that revealed uncomfortable truths. Growth has meant becoming a better version of myself mentally, emotionally, and behaviorally for clarity, presence, and peace.

When the script I was following stopped working, improvisation showed me how to write a new one. The practice taught me to pivot in real time, listen more deeply, and respond with intention rather than reaction. When something wasn't working, I learned to call "New Choice" as an invitation to learn and grow from whatever wasn't serving me.

Personal growth must be a conscious choice. The question isn't whether you have time for development. Instead, ask yourself if you can afford to stay the same.

The Power of Micro-Moments

Growth begins when you stop running old habits on autopilot and often shows up in everyday moments, like:

- Learning from mistakes instead of repeating them
- Communicating with greater clarity and confidence
- Breaking patterns that no longer serve your goals
- Strengthening emotional resilience
- Setting boundaries or embracing new opportunities
- Developing fresh habits, perspectives, or purpose

Over time, these small shifts lead to more profound transformation and lasting fulfillment.

Author James Clear's research in *Atomic Habits: An Easy & Proven Way to Build Good Habits & Break Bad Ones* validates what I discovered through improv: transformation rarely arrives in grand, cinematic breakthroughs. It unfolds through small, deliberate adjustments that, over time, redefine who you are. Clear's "1% better every day" principle mirrors the essence of improvisation: growth built through repetition, awareness, and real-time feedback. Each choice on stage, like each habit in life, compounds into lasting change.

In neuroscience terms, these micro-moments strengthen neural pathways much like rehearsal strengthens muscle memory. The more we practice new choices, the more naturally they become our defaults. That's what improvisation trains: presence, pattern disruption, and adaptability. It's not about perfection; it's about conditioning your brain to pivot toward possibility instead of protection. Every new choice becomes a vote for the person you're becoming. Whether it's speaking up instead of staying silent, pausing instead of reacting, or replacing fear with curiosity, each act, however small, signals progress. Over time, those moments build not only better habits but also a more confident, resilient identity.

Research reinforces this truth. A large-scale study of more than 2,000 college students published in Frontiers in Psychology found that personal growth initiative, the active pursuit of self-improvement, was one of the strongest predictors of purpose, performance, and well-being. Participants who intentionally developed this mindset set clearer goals, made more values-aligned choices, and experienced more consistent progress toward fulfillment.

Growth changes how you live before it changes how you feel.

My Definition, My Beginning

The definition of personal growth varies for each individual. When I think about personal growth, I reflect on all the things I've done to become a better version of myself and to understand myself in relation to others, which also helps me better understand them. Personal growth, for me, has ultimately been rooted in developing emotional intelligence, which I began practicing long before I even understood what it meant. Over the years, my understanding has evolved and expanded through therapy, coaching, reflection, and learning. Growth can be hard to navigate alone. Sometimes you need someone to hold up a mirror and show you what you don't see: those blind spots and areas that need attention.

More broadly, personal growth is the ongoing process of becoming a better version of yourself. It involves expanding your mindset, building new skills, and aligning your actions with your values. Growth happens through self-awareness, adaptability, and the courage to step outside your comfort zone.

A Family of Mindsets: Fixed, Fluid, and Familiar

When I think about growth in those terms, I picture a PowerPoint slide from my "Yes, You Can" keynote speech, where I discuss the distinction between a growth mindset and a fixed mindset.

Psychologist Carol Dweck's research in *Mindset: The New Psychology of Success* revealed something profound: our beliefs about our abilities determine our actual performance. Her distinction between fixed and growth mindsets became my North Star. Every time I called "New Choice" on an old pattern, I was choosing growth mindset over fixed mindset, believing I could develop rather than accepting I was stuck.

On that slide, there's an image of someone holding playing cards, which symbolizes the idea that "these are the cards I've been dealt."

Many people live with the mindset of: "This is just how it is."

What if you could reshuffle the cards? What if you didn't have to accept the hand you were dealt?

That's when I introduce the following image: someone shuffling a deck. I use these two visuals to drive home the point that we can choose differently. We don't have to settle. We can switch tables and find a new card dealer. We can stop letting someone else deal our hand; instead, we can deal ourselves better.

For me, that's what personal development is: the choice to reshuffle the cards.

I love metaphors, and this metaphor runs deep for me. My mom often lived by the "these are the cards I was dealt" mentality. On the other hand, my dad was constantly reshuffling his deck, literally and figuratively.

The contrast of "fixed vs. fluid" didn't just live in theory. It lived in my house.

My dad was a poker player, often in a back room of the flea market where I worked my first job. The difference between being set in one's ways and being open to improvise shaped how I saw myself. I wanted to be as great as my father and better than my mother. Living in such a contradictory environment motivated me to become the best version of me.

The Tools That Shaped Me

Therapy played a massive role in my growth process.

Of course, there are many paths to growth. Some people read books. I own a lot of books (I don't always finish them). I love podcasts. Others pursue continued education, a topic I discuss further in my chapter on learning. For me, it's been a mix of therapy, coaching, reading, listening, improvising, and reflecting.

Podcasting became one of those tools.

Because I craved wisdom from others, I launched *The Pivotal Leader*, my first podcast as producer and host. I interviewed C-suite leaders, CEOs, COOs, CMOs, not just to gain insights, but to grow. Every conversation was like earning an MBA without attending school. I became brighter, sharper, and more intentional about how I presented myself. I also shared that wisdom with others, turning each episode into a ripple effect of growth. Producing a podcast was a strategic business decision for me as well, because it allowed me to build relationships that could potentially turn into client work, especially as a trainer who utilizes improv to develop individuals.

Improv opened those doors to podcasting before it was a thing, as it led me away from accounting to journalism, as you might recall from my chapter about learning. Early in my career, improv helped me realize I wanted to be in broadcast news. I interned in radio and eventually became the news director at my college station. Years later, I missed that world, which led me to using my voice "on the air" in a different way. The success of one show gave me the confidence to produce my second podcast, *Women Your Mother Warned You About*, a space where women in business can discuss work, life, and unapologetic choices. The show ran for five years, nearly 300 episodes, and was just as transformative for me as it was for listeners. Everyone involved personally grew into better individuals, and these shows exemplified the essence of applying the improv principle of "making others look good."

The Therapist, the Mirror, and the Wake-Up Call

My first experience with therapy came after my father died. I'd been mentally preparing for his passing, something I explore more in my chapter on death. In one of my early sessions, the therapist drew a large circle with a smaller one inside of it. He said, "You're living on a toxic island." That visual cracked something open in me. I was in my early 20s, just out of college, and for the first time, I understood that emotional chaos wasn't usual and didn't have to be my reality.

Years later, during my first marriage, my ex and I saw four different counselors. The first session happened because I'd given him back the engagement ring and called off our wedding. The therapist helped us see our emotional triggers and the childhood wounds underneath them, but when his business fell apart, he stopped doing the work. Without two people committed to growth, the relationship collapsed. Plus, I was done when counselor number four pulled out stuffed animals for us to play with.

Eventually, I sought therapy on my own. Before that, I reached out to my business coach, who also happened to be a former pastor. I leaned on him for spiritual guidance (more on that in the chapter on spirituality). He helped me begin planning an exit. Then I found the therapist, Liz, who would give me the tools to love myself again.

In our first session, she asked, *"What's your goal for therapy?"*

I said, *"To choose better next time. I'm not very good at picking good men."*

At the end of the session, she looked at me and said:

"You walk in with so much confidence. But you don't have self-worth."

That hit like a punch to the gut.

I was angry and offended, but I realized she was right. Over time, she helped me understand the difference between confidence, self-esteem, and self-worth, which I later turned into an entire course series. So many people confuse confidence with self-worth. Liz helped me understand I was one of them, and that I wasn't alone.

What Liz identified in me wasn't just a personal blind spot. She showed me a universal human struggle. Research professor Dr. Brené Brown defines shame in *Daring Greatly* as 'the fear of disconnection.' When my therapist pointed out my lack of self-worth, she was naming the shame that kept me from the very connections I craved most.

Eventually, I saw something else even deeper: the problem wasn't just my ex. There was a pattern I hadn't noticed before. I had married someone emotionally like my mother. I was drawn to what was familiar, not what was healthy.

Having that realization put me on a path beyond personal growth. I stopped accepting what I was given and started creating a better life for myself. I learned how to heal.

How Improv Activates Every Element of Personal Growth

Improv did not begin as a self-help tool. For me, it started as curiosity, filled with fun and freedom. I had no idea how profoundly it would shape who I became, both on and off stage.

Personal growth is often discussed in books, workshops, and coaching sessions. Few people mention comedy. Fewer still mention a game like "New Choice". Yet, "New Choice" became one of the most transformational experiences I have ever had. The rules are simple. Step into a scene. When someone yells "new choice," change your response. Try again. Keep moving. Keep creating.

New Choice reprogrammed how I responded to pressure. Perfection lost its grip. Control stopped mattering. I noticed the moments when old habits resurfaced, when tension took over, and when hesitation stole my voice. The game turned into a mirror; one I never expected to face during a pretend scene at rehearsal.

The more I played, the more I noticed fundamental changes. Conversations shifted, patterns softened, and confidence began to build in unexpected places. Improv did not just support growth; it became growth.

I stopped reading about emotional intelligence and started practicing it. Psychologist Daniel Goleman's research in *Emotional Intelligence: Why It Matters More Than IQ* revealed why improv was so transformative for me. The four domains he identifies (self-awareness, self-management, social awareness, and relationship management) are exactly what improv develops. Every scene becomes practice in reading emotions, managing reactions, and responding with empathy.

Deep presence unlocked authentic development. Skills developed naturally without force or pressure. Leadership qualities emerged organically. Communication became more effective. Creativity intensified with each practice session. Every scene functioned as a comprehensive workout, strengthening not physical muscles but the capacity to show up fully and authentically.

Consistent practice created a profound transformation. Not every moment succeeded brilliantly. Many attempts flopped spectacularly. Failure became familiar territory, eventually even welcome. Every misstep provided valuable feedback. Every adjustment trained my brain to respond thoughtfully instead of impulsively, to adapt fluidly instead of freezing under pressure.

Improvisation taught me to change through movement, not analysis. Transformation happened through deliberate action, one slight pivot at a time.

A growth mindset requires flexibility. Improv demands it. Control never lasted long in a scene. Curiosity always did. When I stopped trying to win and started building with others, collaboration came naturally. Play created freedom. Freedom made room for better choices.

Emotion once felt like a disruption. In improv, emotion became information. I learned to read cues, my partner's tone, and my own nervous system. My presence stayed intact, even when chaos entered the room. That ability is carried into daily life, meetings, relationships, and conflict.

Improvisation offered more than performance skills. Every scene became a doorway to the future version of myself. The one I used to talk about. The one I hoped would show up someday.

Growth happened through play. Practice. Repetition. Courage.

Every new choice taught me the same lesson. Change never asks for perfection. Change asks for participation. Say something new. Take the risk. Try again.

Personal development is not theory. Personal development is practice.

Make the New Choice Real: Practices for Becoming

Personal growth is a lived practice, not another worksheet to download from social media. You learn and grow by doing, reflecting, adjusting, and trying again. I love going into organizations and watching growth reveal itself in real time through a few improv exercises.

Another mantra in the improv world is "Don't talk about it. Do something." Action beats explanation every day, all day. Scenes (and life) are more powerful when you show rather than tell. The improv stage taught me that growth isn't just about skill-building. Improvising is about presence, play, and giving yourself permission to make new choices.

Here's how to take what you've read and put it into motion:

Scene Work:

Take the stage and move from theory to practice with these quick drills to help you catch your defaults, pivot in the moment, and train your brain for change.

- Mirror Moment Practice: Stand in front of a mirror for 60 seconds daily. Notice your presence without judgment. Ask: "What energy am I bringing today?" Speak one truth aloud.

- New Choice Flash Round: Pick one area where you feel stuck. Write your default response, then quickly write three new possible choices without editing or overthinking.

- Confidence vs. Self-Worth Mapping: Draw two columns. List five ways confidence and self-worth each show up in your life. Identify what's missing and what you want to strengthen.

Side Coaching:

Before making more choices, pause and check in. The following prompts will help you be honest about what's on autopilot and what needs to change.

- What's one "mirror moment" that made you see yourself differently?

- Where have you mistaken confidence for self-worth in your life?

- What emotional pattern are you ready to stop repeating, and what would a new choice look like?

Script Revision:

Every rehearsal ends with a new line to carry forward. Try this one on and let it guide your next decision:

> *"Past patterns do not bind me. Each moment is a chance to choose again and grow by listening, learning, and letting go."*

Encore: Growth Is the Practice of Becoming

Personal growth demands self-reflection, conscious effort, and willingness to change repeatedly. Every choice becomes an opportunity to evolve, which rarely occurs under ideal circumstances. Growth doesn't happen during polished, Instagram-worthy moments. Instead, transformation occurs when you don't know what to say next but speak anyway, feel broken but walk into the therapy office regardless, or when you hear "New Choice" and summon courage to try again, whether onstage or in real life.

Growth isn't linear. Growth is layered, messy, and deeply personal. It's built in the quiet moments when no one is cheering, and progress feels like standing still. That's where grit comes in. Psychologist

Angela Duckworth's research in *Grit: The Power of Passion and Perseverance* reveals that long-term achievement depends less on talent and more on sustained effort over time. Her findings echo what my own life has proven: real transformation requires showing up long after the initial spark of motivation fades.

My journey through therapy, failed relationships, and career pivots wasn't about innate skill or perfect timing; it was about persistence when nothing seemed to be changing. It meant trusting that every small act of courage, each boundary set, each truth spoken, each "new choice" made was building strength beneath the surface. Growth, like grit, lives in the repetition of showing up.

Improvisation, especially the game "New Choice," taught me that change doesn't have to feel terrifying. Development can be creative, empowering, and genuinely enjoyable because growth isn't merely theoretical – it's practiced. Growth is the act of stepping in again and again, adjusting, refining, and allowing yourself to evolve through the process.

The benefits extend far beyond temporary feelings of well-being. People who actively engage in personal development don't just build self-awareness; they construct clear direction for their lives. Research demonstrates that growth-minded individuals tend to set clearer goals, create specific life plans, perform academically and professionally, recover faster from setbacks, and make more consistent, values-aligned choices throughout their lives.

A growth mindset never happens accidentally or through fortunate circumstances. Genuine development requires intentional commitment. I didn't read about growth in books and suddenly transform. I lived it actively through marriages and divorces, boardrooms and therapy sessions, improv stages and podcast interviews. Every moment I chose to reflect, rewrite, risk, or release something, I expanded who I was becoming.

Harness the power of improvising your way forward. Scripts aren't necessary. Willingness to listen deeply, trust yourself completely, and make one new choice simultaneously creates transformation.

Growth isn't perfection. Growth is presence. Growth is practice.

You're not stuck in old patterns. You're actively becoming someone new.

Script Notes: Rewriting My Growth Story

These are the choices that redefined my relationship with myself. Use them as fuel to spark your own turning points.

1. Saying Yes to Therapy Before I Had the Words for It

After my dad died, I didn't know what I needed, but I walked into a therapist's office anyway. My decision to choose therapy cracked me open, giving me language, tools, and space to feel.

2. Handing Back the Engagement Ring

I knew deep down the marriage wasn't right. Returning that ring wasn't just an act of courage. I empowered myself to use my voice and choose myself, even though I eventually, and wrongfully, decided to marry him. I am a better person because of all the choices I made in that relationship.

3. Naming the Pattern I Didn't Want to Repeat

The day I said out loud, "I married a version of my mother," was the day I stopped pretending. That moment let me grieve what was and start building something new.

4. Choosing a Therapist Who Challenged Me

When my therapist said, "You have confidence, but not self-worth," I could've walked out. Instead, I stayed. That choice gave me clarity I didn't know I needed.

5. Turning Improv into a Personal Development Playground

What started as a creative outlet became my greatest growth accelerator. I chose to see the stage as more than a performance. I saw it for what it really was: a practice for real life.

6. Launching a Podcast to Learn Out Loud

I didn't wait for permission or perfection. I interviewed leaders, asked hard questions, and turned curiosity into connection. The mic became a mirror for my own development.

7. Choosing to Reshuffle My Deck

Instead of accepting "these are the cards I was dealt," I chose to reshuffle, over and over again, sometimes winning, sometimes losing. I stopped playing the hand I hated and dealt myself a new one, on my terms.

Chapter 12
Choosing How To Heal

Listening to Your Body's Truth

"If you do not take care of yourself, the responsibility falls on someone else, and that's a burden you don't want to leave behind." — Gloria Steinem

Health Is Wealth (And Most of Us Are in Emotional Debt)

I used to roll my eyes at the phrase "health is wealth." It felt like something you'd see on a yoga mat or hear from a wellness influencer with perfect lighting. The older I get, the more I feel the truth of it in my bones, literally.

When your body runs low, everything else suffers: your mindset, your energy, your ability to show up and make meaningful choices. Every new choice needs fuel, and that fuel is your health. Energy, clarity, and strength all begin there. Health is a scene partner you can't ignore in a lifetime of new choices to manage.

No one else can play your role, as I am often reminded of in my profession as a speaker and trainer. Yet we often neglect our health, treating it like a background character, pushing through symptoms, skipping maintenance, hoping the understudy can carry the load.

We delay appointments. We downplay symptoms. We tell ourselves we're fine. Sometimes we're scared of what we'll find out. Sometimes we're scared we'll be judged. Sometimes, we've been dismissed so many times, we stop asking altogether.

Let's be honest: most of us aren't avoiding the doctor because we're too busy. We're avoiding the doctor because we're afraid. Afraid of being told something we don't want to hear. Fearful of being gaslit. Scared of being taken seriously and then having to deal with the reality. In a 2019 BMJ Open study, fear of diagnosis, especially cancer, was named one of the top reasons people avoid care, even when symptoms are present. Another study from the Cleveland Clinic found that 65% of men delay doctor visits, and more than a third withhold critical information out of shame or fear of being seen as weak.

People with higher BMIs report avoiding appointments because of weight-based judgment or humiliation. Individuals with anxiety or depression often delay treatment out of fear they'll be labeled "unstable." According to the World Health Organization, up to 60% of people with mental illness go untreated, not because care is unavailable, but because judgment makes it feel unsafe.

This creates a vicious loop: Avoid care ⇨ symptoms worsen ⇨ shame deepens ⇨ avoid care even more.

What breaks us is the belief that we're already broken. Our biggest challenge is psychological.

Access to care is a privilege not afforded to all, but it doesn't always lead to action. A 2022 Kaiser Family Foundation study revealed that 25% of insured Americans still skip care due to cost or systemic fatigue. Worse, only 8% of adults in the U.S. consistently practice all five of the most recommended healthy behaviors: not smoking, maintaining a healthy weight, exercising regularly, eating a balanced diet, and limiting alcohol use.

We know these behaviors improve longevity, reduce disease, and enhance quality of life, yet most struggle with consistent implementation. The barrier isn't just knowledge about benefits, but the reality of confronting fear, overcoming fatigue, and managing the emotional resistance that accompanies meaningful change.

Reality check: 92% of us know what we should do for our health, yet we consistently fail.

The gap between knowledge and action isn't about willpower or laziness. Fear, overwhelm, and decision fatigue occupy the space between knowing and doing. Health decisions carry profound emotional weight that rarely gets acknowledged.

We choose fast food not because it's cheaper but because it feels safer and more familiar. We avoid medical screenings not because we think invincible but because we're terrified of potential discoveries. We skip workouts not because we're unmotivated but because our nervous system interprets physical discomfort as genuine danger.

Many destructive health habits function as protective responses masquerading as comfort choices.

Health requires deeply personal, emotional navigation that operates more like improvisation than prescription. We crave quick fixes, definitive checklists, and linear progress. Real wellness emerges through the accumulation of micro-decisions, strategic pivots, and uncomfortable confrontations with the truth. Listening to your body's signals, asking better questions, and making a "New Choice" with your health requires genuine courage.

Improvisation taught me to stop avoiding reality and remain present, curious, and adaptable when facing uncertainty. The practice also empowered me to speak up when feeling silenced, advocate when feeling dismissed, and pivot when no script existed to follow.

When healthcare systems change too slowly, you can and should call "New Choice" immediately.

When the Prescription Doesn't Fit, Rewrite the Script

My concerns about health started earlier than I realized. When I think about it now, it may go all the way back to childhood, age 12, when my father had a series of congestive heart failures.

Even before that, I remember negotiating with a doctor not to remove my tonsils because I declared I felt fine. As a kid, I didn't understand why things were happening to me, like frequent blood tests and unexplained symptoms. The lack of understanding became a trauma that stuck with me for decades.

Watching my father's health deteriorate shaped how I viewed the medical world. My mother did everything she could to care for him. She micromanaged his diet, his appointments, everything.

No matter what she did, we were in and out of hospitals constantly until he passed away when I was 22. That experience planted a deep belief in me that sometimes, even when you do everything "right," it's not enough.

Years later, when my mother ended up in the ICU with an aortic aneurysm, I had to become her advocate. The doctors were exhausted, overworked, and often lacked the ability to empathize as they once did. One dentist even came into her room, suggesting they remove all of her teeth before surgery, with no explanation or consideration for how terrifying that sounded to my mother. I noticed her flinching every time the hospital door shut. Through this observation, I learned that she was claustrophobic. No one paid attention, thus no one asked, except for me. Not because she was my mom, but because improv had taught me how to study non-verbal behavior.

Advocacy became my survival skill. I had to be her voice when she was too scared or too sick to speak for herself. Shortly after that, I became the patient.

I had been traveling a lot, especially to see my mother, and I started having breathing issues. I went to an urgent care facility because I thought I was having a heart attack. The doctor dismissed me by asking me if I knew what a panic attack was. I knew what a panic attack felt like because I've experienced them before. My explanations fell on deaf ears. They x-rayed my lungs, gave me a blood test, and sent me on my way. They only forgot to say "Don't call us, we'll call you" as the automatic sliding exit door closed abruptly behind me. I went home, still struggling to breathe with a high resting heart rate of 150, praying I wouldn't die. Little did I know how close death was.

A few days later, a nurse called me and left me a voicemail advising me to get to a hospital immediately. I needed an emergency blood transfusion. For two days, I lay in a hospital bed receiving five bags of blood in one arm while they took blood from the other arm to test it. They released me with no explanation or directions other than "see your primary caregiver in two weeks." I refused to leave without seeing a doctor again so that I could understand my condition. He refused to come to my hospital room and called me instead. I was absolutely terrified and in disbelief at what I had just endured. I was processed like a customer at the grocery store. When I asked what I should do if this happened to me again, the doctor flippantly said, "Come back for another transfusion."

That was the beginning of my unexplained anemia. No one had answers beyond the most common tests that they knew how to dispense. I was poked, scanned, scoped, and dismissed. I even flew to another city for other tests because I lost trust in the doctors near me after one of the tests led to septic shock. For nine years, I took an iron pill every day and pretended I was fine.

Until it happened again.

This time, I used my improv mindset.

I demanded a referral. I sought out a teaching hospital. I asked deeper questions. I shared my full story. Finally, I found a doctor who listened, was curious, and put together the puzzle pieces.

During the writing of this book, we are on a new journey with answers and solutions because I started teaching a medical practitioner how to be curious with me.

It's ironic, really. My health journey led me to medical improv. I now train doctors and nurses on how to be better listeners, show empathy, and engage with curiosity instead of rushing to judgment because I've lived the consequences of what happens when they don't.

Even recently, dental health became a source of trauma for me. I avoided going until an infection forced my hand. I needed major work, but I'm different now. I speak up. I disclose my anxiety. I ask for options. I don't settle for "this is just how it is." This scenario is happening in real time as I write. The ability for me to face fear has been fueled by improv. Instead of getting on stage and possibly failing, I get into a dentist's chair and declare what I need to feel safe.

My husband has dealt with his own health issues, and like me, he digs for answers. We are an exception. Most people accept what they're told. Most people feel disempowered, dismissed, or afraid.

This chapter is an invitation to see your health not as a fixed outcome, but as a dynamic, evolving relationship with your body, your choices, your providers, and your courage to call "New Choice" when something doesn't feel right. Your job is not to be perfect. Your job is to stay present, ask questions, and keep showing up for your own care.

No one else will do it better than you can, once you decide to advocate for yourself like your life depends on it.

Because it does.

Fear around healthcare doesn't come out of nowhere. For many, that fear is earned and built from years of feeling dismissed, misdiagnosed, or unheard. The system itself often reinforces avoidance. When trust is broken repeatedly, even the act of making an appointment can feel like a risk. Understanding the data matters, not just to prove a point, but to validate the lived experience so many carry silently. Research confirms what the body already knows: the system is hard to trust, which is exactly why learning to trust yourself becomes essential.

Health, Fear, and the Art of New Choice

Avoidance doesn't always stem from neglect or ignorance. More often, it begins with fear, an emotion that rarely travels alone. Shame, overwhelm, and uncertainty follow close behind, whispering reminders of past experiences where care was delayed, dismissed, or denied.

Many people carry the weight of past medical experiences, not in charts, but in their bodies. Tight shoulders respond to a skeptical glance. Tears fall during routine checkups without warning. Words meant to advocate stay locked in the throat, swallowed before they can be spoken. The body remembers what the mind tries to move past.

Patterns accumulate gradually. Care gets postponed. Symptoms intensify. Shame compounds the problem. The cycle perpetuates itself endlessly. Self-protection mechanisms drive such behaviors rather than laziness or indifference.

Fear-based avoidance of medical care has been well documented. In a 2015 national study by the Journal of General Internal Medicine, people reported avoiding care due to anxiety, shame, prior negative experiences, and fear of judgment, even when insured and resourced. Similar patterns appear in a 2014 review by BMC Medical Ethics, where shame in healthcare emerged as a significant, yet often invisible, barrier.

When Access Doesn't Equal Trust

Coverage alone doesn't guarantee usage. Trust remains a separate currency, and it is much harder to earn.

Studies show a wide range, between 20% and 80%, of people in the U.S. report some level of distrust in the healthcare system (American Journal of Public Health). This distrust correlates strongly with worse self-reported health outcomes, regardless of access or income.

Even with good insurance, many patients delay appointments or minimize symptoms. Health care becomes a stage where patients feel pressure to perform: to sound credible, not dramatic; to appear compliant, not inconvenient. Those with chronic, invisible, or hard-to-pinpoint conditions often feel gaslit instead of guided. Over time, questions dry up. People stop asking. They "push through." They wait until the concern becomes a crisis. By then, care becomes harder, more expensive, and more traumatic.

Curiosity often goes unrewarded in medical settings. Yet curiosity is what most patients need more of, and what the system needs most from its providers.

The Real Barrier to Behavior Change

Information alone doesn't spark change. Emotions do. Health decisions often come from fear, fatigue, or frustration, not logic. Rationalization usually follows action, not the other way around.

In behavioral science, this disconnect is known as the intention-behavior gap, a well-documented phenomenon where strong intentions fail to translate into consistent action. Meta-analyses by the European Review of Social Psychology show that while intentions and behaviors are correlated, intentions typically explain only about 23% to 28% of actual behavior.

Even when people genuinely want to improve their health (eat better, move more, ask better questions), they often don't follow through. Environmental triggers, emotional load, and ingrained patterns override good intentions. For example, a 2006 analysis by Psychological Bulletin found that even high motivation only modestly increases follow-through on health behaviors like exercise or diet.

Neuroscience offers part of the explanation. When the nervous system perceives a physical or emotional threat, it prioritizes safety over progress. Discomfort, even when healthy, can register as danger. A skipped workout, avoided screening, or fast-food fallback often reflects a brain trying to soothe, not sabotage.

According to the Morbidity and Mortality Weekly Report, only 27.5% of adults globally meet physical activity guidelines, and fewer than 20% consume the recommended servings of fruits and vegetables. These numbers speak less to a knowledge deficit and more to a systems and behavior challenge.

Bridging the gap between intention and action requires more than willpower. It demands a supportive environment, emotional regulation, clear planning, and permission to pivot when old strategies no longer work.

Making new choices begins here, not as a dramatic overhaul, but as a quiet decision to try again with presence, flexibility, and curiosity.

Where New Choice Comes In

A New Choice begins with noticing. Noticing the twitch of hesitation, the edge of resistance, the tightness in your chest that says, "Something doesn't feel right." That moment holds power. One breath. One question. One more courageous word than usual. Movement begins there.

Autopilot serves until it doesn't. Routines offer relief until they dull your awareness. Healing requires flexibility, not perfection. Health unfolds as a conversation, one between your body, your environment, and the part of you willing to stay present long enough to listen.

Plans can change. Providers can be replaced. Approaches can be reimagined. Permission already lives inside you. No announcement necessary.

The Improv Mindset for Health

Among all life's variables, health demands the most adaptability.

The body evolves like a landscape, weathered by time, shaped by emotion, responding to unseen forces. Yesterday's solution might become today's strain. Familiar choices lose their effectiveness, yet many cling to them out of habit or fear.

"New Choice" breaks the cycle. Crisis isn't required as a catalyst. Certainty isn't a prerequisite for action. Awareness and willingness to respond create the opening for change.

Improv taught me to stop performing for the white coat. Each appointment became an invitation to collaborate. Passive silence gave way to active participation. Some providers leaned in. Others resisted. Either way, I stopped shrinking myself to fit into someone else's frame.

That shift revealed the cracks: empathy missing from the dialogue, burnout etched into faces, rushed conversations where listening once lived. Disconnection disguised as efficiency.

Bringing humanity back into the room started with mine.

Ways To Improv Your Health

Now that you've heard my story, let's turn inward. Where are you avoiding? Where are you already advocating? Let's improvise our way through it with the following exercises.

Scene Work:

Take the stage and move from theory to practice with these quick drills to help you catch your defaults, pivot in the moment, and train your brain for change.

- "Yes, And" Your Health History: Write about a frustrating health experience. Retell it using "Yes, And": "Yes, that happened, and here's what I learned" or "Yes, I was afraid, and I showed up anyway."

- Call "New Choice" on One Health Habit: Identify one current health routine, habit, or mindset that no longer serves you. Ask: "What's one small new choice I can make today?" Write it down and do it.

- Practice Medical Advocacy: Role-play or practice saying, "Can you walk me through that?" "What are the other possibilities?" "What questions should I be asking?" or "Can we slow down for a moment?"

Side Coaching:

Before making more choices, pause and check in. The following prompts will help you be honest about what's on autopilot and what needs to change.

- What patterns do you notice in responding to physical discomfort or health concerns?

- What small health signals have you been ignoring, and why?

- How does curiosity feel different from fear regarding your body and health?

Script Revision:

Every rehearsal ends with a new line to carry forward. Try this one on and let it guide your next decision:

> *"I don't need to have it all figured out. I stay present, curious, and courageous enough to call New Choice when it matters most."*

Encore: Reclaiming Your Voice in the Conversation of Care

Health is a conversation, not a checklist. For most of us, it's a conversation we've avoided, misunderstood, or been shut out of at some point. But every moment you listen to your body, ask a new question, or speak up for yourself is a moment you take the lead in that conversation.

You don't need to have the perfect words. You don't need to know exactly what to do. You just need to be willing to stay present when things get uncertain.

Improv has taught me to stay curious and make new and unexpected choices.

The system is rarely designed to support our voices, but that doesn't mean you should stop speaking. Instead, get louder, clearer, and more curious. Stop apologizing for taking up space in exam rooms and in your own body.

You are allowed to outgrow old routines. You are allowed to change doctors. You are allowed to walk into a room and expect to be treated with dignity.

When the script no longer fits, permission exists to pivot. Call "New Choice," not just once, but whenever the old rhythm no longer supports you. Write a new preSCRIPTion that reflects what your body is asking for now.

Health stories are co-created with presence, persistence, and the courage to begin again.

No fixed formula applies to every chapter. Like any meaningful relationship, your connection to your body will evolve. Some days bring clarity. Others ask questions. Each moment offers a cue: a symptom, a sensation, or a story waiting to be heard.

A single shift can spark momentum. A sharper question can shift the tone. A braver choice can reopen what once felt closed.

"New Choice" doesn't demand reinvention. Instead, it requires a willingness to stay awake, stay curious, and stay in the scene, especially when the next step remains unclear.

Script Notes: Reclaiming My Health Story

Here are the choices that redefined how I show up for my body, my care, and myself. Use them as inspiration to make your own "New Choice" moments.

1. Speaking Up at Urgent Care: When I was dismissed as anxious, I calmly said, "My symptoms aren't anxiety-related. I know my body." The choice got me a blood test and an emergency transfusion that may have saved my life.

2. Demanding a Referral: I stopped waiting for permission and asked for a specialist. My persistence led me to a doctor who listened, asked better questions, and finally started putting the pieces together.

3. Flying to Another City: I didn't trust the answers I was getting locally. I flew across the country to keep searching. Radical self-belief and a refusal to settle for uncertainty drove the choice.

4. Advocating for My Mother: I asked what no one else noticed in the ICU: "Why does she flinch every time the door shuts?" My observation revealed her claustrophobia and reminded me of the importance of observation, not just assumption.

5. Naming My Anxiety at the Dentist: I told the truth: "I have high anxiety. What can we do about it?" Honesty opened up options I didn't know existed and turned a dreaded visit into a manageable plan.

6. Saying "No More Guessing": After years of band-aid solutions, I stopped accepting vague answers. Persistence transformed me from a passive patient into a determined advocate.

Chapter 13

Choosing A Spiritual Path

Reclaiming Faith, Doubt, and a Practice That Fits

"The spiritual journey is individual, highly personal. It can have no formula." — Stephen Levine

The church pew was hard, the sermon long, and by the third hour, I was whisper-squirming in my uncle's ear: "How much longer?" At nine years old, I sat through a four-hour Seventh Day Adventist service, convinced that if this was religion, I wanted no part of it. That was my first real New Choice moment with religion, and it shaped how I would think about faith for decades to come.

Some people find comfort in religion. Others identify as spiritual, without subscribing to a specific doctrine. Some reject the idea of a higher power altogether, choosing atheism.

I chose the word *spirituality* for this chapter because it leaves space for you. Wherever you are on your journey, or wherever you've been, this chapter invites you to explore. Not to land on one definitive label, but to pause, look around, and ask: *What do I believe? And where did that belief come from?*

You may have stood in multiple places throughout your life. I know many people who have. One friend of mine grew up deeply Christian, fully immersed in the traditions of his faith. In his 20s, after years of studying evolution and science, he became a devout atheist. My stepson leans that way too, not from study, but from influence. His mother and stepfather are strong atheists, and despite growing up exposed to Christianity in our home, his current belief reflects the environment he's most immersed in.

Belief is rarely static. Pew Research shows that nearly 30% of Americans identify as religiously unaffiliated, a dramatic rise from just a decade ago. And 28% of U.S. adults have left the religion in which they were raised. That tells us something big: people are shifting. They're seeking.

They're permitting themselves to change.

When it comes to faith, whether it's full of conviction or full of questions, many of us stay stuck in stories handed to us. We inherit beliefs and build identities around them, sometimes without realizing we've outgrown them. Other times, we cling tightly out of fear. What if questioning means losing our foundation? What if changing our minds makes us wrong?

Improv has taught me something life-changing: we are always allowed to choose again.

In improv, when a scene stalls or doesn't feel right, we call out *"New choice!"* The New Choice exercise is a tool that invites us into something more interesting, and often the better choice.

Imagine giving yourself the same grace in your spiritual life.

This chapter isn't here to tell you what to believe. Instead, this chapter is here to help you get curious about how to think while feeling free to explore, experiment, and change directions on your terms.

Clarifying Definitions of Spirituality, Religion, and Atheism

Spirituality, religion, and atheism might appear to be very different paths. At their core, though, each one reflects a search for meaning, belonging, and truth.

Spirituality often begins as an inner pull, a quiet question, a sense of connection that doesn't require a building, a book, or a label. Some people feel this through nature, music, meditation, or even a deep breath that brings unexpected peace. Spirituality doesn't follow a script. The connection is often fluid and personal, guided more by curiosity than by rules.

Religion tends to provide structure. Traditions, texts, rituals, and shared beliefs offer a clear framework for understanding the divine and living in service to others. Many people are drawn to religion for its community, consistency, and purpose. Faith in this form becomes a way of life, shaped by generations before.

Atheism reflects a belief that no god or higher power exists. That doesn't mean an absence of values. Many atheists live with compassion, clarity, and conviction, grounded in reason, science, or human ethics. For some, the lack of belief creates a more profound commitment to the present moment and to one another.

People move between these categories more often than most assume. Some stay rooted. Others explore, blend, or leave. Belief rarely follows a straight line. Culture, childhood, education, and personal experience all influence the evolution of beliefs. Faith, or the absence of it, grows and shifts over time. Rather than being a destination, belief becomes a living process, one that continues to evolve as we do.

How I Chose My Religion ... Twice.

I wasn't baptized as a baby, which is unusual in Catholicism. My parents gave my brother and me the option to choose our religion when I was in fourth grade, and he was in second grade. To this day, I still don't understand why they made that decision or how it came about. All I know is that they wanted us to switch from a public elementary school to a Catholic elementary school for a better education, and we couldn't enroll until we completed catechism classes, which were similar to Sunday school classes but held on Saturdays so that we could learn the basics of the Bible.

But let me back up.

My father was Catholic, and my mother was a Seventh-day Adventist. That part alone is wild, especially considering our German heritage. Most Germans are raised Lutheran. Somehow, my mother's side practiced a religion that, during World War II, nearly got them killed. What many don't realize is that even Germans were imprisoned in internment camps. My mother's family was among them. Some of the religious customs of Seventh-day Adventists, such as observing the Sabbath from sundown on Friday to sundown on Saturday, abstaining from pork and shellfish, and refraining from activities like alcohol consumption and tattooing, mirror Jewish practices. At one point, German soldiers assumed my mother and her family members were Jewish. They were nearly executed because of that, but when my grandfather dropped to his knees to pray, the Nazi soldiers put their guns down.

Growing up, I saw the contradictions of my mother's beliefs firsthand. She couldn't go out on Friday nights because of the Sabbath, even though she was captain of the cheerleading team. She wasn't supposed to drink or smoke, but she did both. Growing up, having pierced ears was not allowed, so of course I wanted them. Her strict rules clashed with her behavior, which made things even more confusing for me.

When it came time to choose a religion, it felt like a big decision, especially for a kid, but I tried to approach it logically, in true nine-year-old fashion. I figured I should give the Seventh-day Adventist Church a try, so I went with my uncle, my mom's brother. Not my mom. (Still don't know where she was in all this.)

The service was four hours long. Four. Hours. That was enough for me to decide, "Yeah, no thanks." Additionally, I was closer to my dad's side of the family, and we had already attended the Catholic Church for the major holidays. It made more sense socially and emotionally to align with them.

Just like that, I became Catholic. I received the most significant childhood sacraments: baptism, First Communion, and Confirmation. I attended both Catholic elementary school and Catholic high school, as well as a Jesuit college. Interestingly, I'm pursuing my master's degree at a Christian-based university, not Catholic this time, but still aligned with a faith-based foundation.

For a long time, I thought I understood my faith, but I didn't really get what it meant to be a Christian, or what the Bible said, until much later.

I lost my way with Catholicism after one deeply personal experience. I share more about it in the financial chapter, but the short version is this: I was the victim of a con artist, and I met him in church. A Catholic church. When I realized what was happening, I reached out to the priest for help. He refused to get involved. That broke me. I lost my faith in the Church. I lost my faith in Christ. And I walked away, for a long time.

Eventually, I moved to a new city with my fiancé, who would later become my husband, and we began visiting churches. We first visited the local Catholic church, but something was missing. We explored other options. Living in the Bible Belt meant there was a church on nearly every corner. We began visiting non-denominational and Protestant churches, just trying to find a good fit.

Something started to shift.

For the first time in my life, I began to understand Christianity. Not just the rituals, but the relationship. The meaning behind the stories. The teachings of Jesus. Within a couple of years, I decided to get baptized again, this time as a born-again Christian. I publicly declared that I was giving my life to Christ.

My fiancé became my first husband, and he wasn't thrilled with my decision. He told me point-blank that he didn't want me to expect him to do the same. His discomfort revealed something more profound: he didn't have a strong enough foundation of faith to feel secure or open to the experience, and that was okay because my faith walk was mine, not his.

Still, it wasn't easy. I was battling health issues. My mother had gotten sick just a few months after my baptism, and I was diagnosed with anemia shortly after. My marriage was unraveling. Even though I had this renewed faith, I was stuck on what it meant to be a biblical wife. I believed I had to "stick it out" in a bad marriage, no matter what.

During that time, I was working with a business coach who had previously served as a pastor for over 30 years. One day, I broke down over coffee, sharing how miserable I was. I told him I was torn between my faith and my failing marriage.

He looked me in the eye and asked, "Would Christ, your Father, want his daughter to be this unhappy?"

That question cracked something open in me. "No," I said. "I don't think He would."

"Of course not," he said. "If you've tried everything, it's time for you to go."

That moment shifted how I understood scripture. It gave me a more compassionate and realistic perspective on what it means to live according to one's faith. I learned that being a biblical wife doesn't mean suffering endlessly. It means honoring yourself, your health, and your relationship with God.

Since then, my faith has been a constant, not a cure-all but a foundation. My belief in Christ has carried me through the hardest seasons and has been a source of celebration in the best ones. To me, being a Christian is about striving to be the best version of myself, not just for myself but for the people I'm here to serve and support.

When I started dating again after my divorce, finding a godly man was at the top of my list. On my first phone call with the man who would become my husband, he asked me out for Sunday dinner. When he asked what I'd be doing that day, I said, "I'm going to church." That was my litmus test. His response? "Can I come with you?"

That told me everything I needed to know.

He wasn't attending church at the time, but his faith was strong. Since then, we've walked that journey together. Sharing a faithful life with someone who values it too has been powerful.

In case you're wondering about the improv piece, yes, improv had a role in all of this. After moving to a new city and trying to find my footing again, improv helped me reconnect to myself. It reminded me that no matter what, I could always call *"New Choice"*, even in matters of the soul.

The Evolving Landscape of Belief

Belief isn't one-size-fits-all. For many people, faith is a winding path marked by exploration, challenge, and discovery. Often, what we believe doesn't stay the same.

Faith can be something we inherit, but that doesn't mean it remains untouched. We grow, we learn, we experience pain, transformation, joy, and loss. All of it, every high and low, can shift how we see the world and what we believe about it.

Education plays a decisive role in that shift. According to the General Social Survey (GSS), higher levels of education often correlate with lower levels of affiliation with organized religion. The more we learn, the more we question. It's no surprise that education can shake the scaffolding of faith. Knowing more doesn't kill belief. Sometimes it just makes the questions louder. Walking away from an institution doesn't necessarily mean walking away from meaning. Many people who leave traditional religion still identify as spiritual but not religious. They ask deeper questions, turn inward, and explore mindfulness, philosophy, and the connection between them. In many cases, knowledge deepens or reshapes belief.

Upbringing, too, leaves a deep imprint. A 2016 study from Barna Group found that parents are the most significant influence on a child's spiritual worldview, as was the case with me. Those beliefs may evolve over time, but the foundation often begins at home. My own stepson is a perfect example. His current beliefs lean toward atheism, not because of any single defining moment, but rather due to consistent exposure to that perspective through his mother and stepfather. Even though he's also seen a different kind of faith modeled in our home, his worldview reflects where he's been most influenced.

The influence doesn't end with family. Faith doesn't live in a vacuum. Faith is shaped in the spaces we share, in friendships, late-night conversations, family dinners, and text threads. Our beliefs often mirror the people we do life with. A 2010 study published in the American Sociological Review found that our spiritual and religious views tend to align with those in our closest social circles. It makes sense. When we're surrounded by questioners, we question more.

When believers surround us, we may lean in or feel the pressure to stay. Either way, our communities color our convictions. We're wired for belonging. Sometimes, we adopt the values around us to stay connected. Sometimes we reject them to find ourselves.

Often, we do a bit of both.

Despite what headlines may suggest, spirituality is far from fading. A 2023 Gallup poll found that 75% of Americans still believe in some form of higher power. They may not sit in pews or follow a specific doctrine, but their desire for connection, purpose, and something greater remains. They are still seeking.

That's why I use the word *spirituality* in this chapter. My intention was not to box anyone in or exclude anyone, but to open a door wide enough for everyone (religious, atheist, curious, unsure) to walk through. Belief is a process, a practice, and a choice we get to make repeatedly.

The Role of Improv in My Spiritual Journey

Improv has quietly guided me through my spiritual path, not as a doctrine, but as a mindset and has shown up in the form of curiosity, collaboration, and community, long before I ever connected the dots.

At its core, improv teaches us the principles of staying open, listening deeply, and responding without judgment, which has helped me navigate my faith.

I never stopped asking questions. I stayed curious. I explored different belief systems until I found one that felt aligned, not just in terms of theology, but also in terms of belonging. For me, spirituality was about choosing both Christianity and community in a space where I felt seen, connected, and supported. Improv became my spiritual practice - a quiet chapel of presence, listening, and shared breath.

In fact, over the years, many people have jokingly referred to my improv theater as *"The Church of Improv."* At first, I thought that was weird, but honestly, it fits. Our space has always drawn people from all walks of life: extreme liberals and staunch conservatives, Christians and atheists, people in their 20s and people in their 70s. My improv theater is one of the only places I've ever witnessed such radically different people come together and truly accept one another, because the culture is grounded in the 'Yes, And' principle: acceptance without judgment.

Improv invites you to sit beside someone else's truth without needing to rearrange the furniture. The improv mindset has rewired how I see the world. Following these principles is a practice of grace, and in many ways, it mirrors the foundation of my faith. From a Christian perspective, at least in my experience, Christ accepts all sinners, regardless of what they've done or what they believe. I've met plenty of atheists whose values and compassion would put many religious people to shame. I've also known believers who forget that acceptance is a commandment, not a suggestion.

Improv reminds me to drop the judgment and stay human.

One of the most pivotal moments in my spiritual journey occurred during the early days of the COVID pandemic. I was going through a divorce. The world felt like it was falling apart. In the midst of that storm, I reached out to my business coach and the former pastor and had one of the most important conversations of my life. Our exchange and my willingness to ask for support and listen deeply came from my improv training. I was reminded that we're not meant to figure everything out on our own.

I forgot to mention in my earlier story how vital my church group was during that season. Belonging to that group helped me hold on to my faith when everything else felt shaky. Having a sense of community, the kind that listens, encourages, and holds space for uncertainty, was a direct reflection of what I've always practiced through improv.

Improv taught me to collaborate, to say "Yes" to others' ideas, even when I didn't have the answers, to stay curious about different perspectives, and to believe that no matter how messy the scene gets, there's always room to pivot.

In improv, we say *"New choice!"* when something isn't working. I've said that to myself, quietly and courageously, many times throughout my spiritual life. Each time, it's led me closer to something real.

Exercises To Improv Your Soul

Take a breath before you move forward. You've just walked through a story of questions, pivots, and personal truth. What follows is an opportunity to explore your own. These prompts are designed to help you listen closely to yourself, without pressure to define everything.

Scene Work:

Take the stage and move from theory to practice with these quick drills to help you catch your defaults, pivot in the moment, and train your brain for change.

- New Choice Belief Edition: Write down three spiritual/religious beliefs from your upbringing. Next to each, write a "New Choice" version that aligns more with who you are now.

- "Yes, And" Your Inner Voice: Take a spiritual question or doubt you've been having. Respond using "Yes, And" to accept the uncertainty and build possibility from there.

- Improvise Your Practice: For one week, try a different spiritual practice each day based on pure curiosity: light a candle, walk in nature, sing, write a letter to the divine, or sit in silence.

Side Coaching:

Before making more choices, pause and check in. The following prompts will help you be honest about what's on autopilot and what needs to change.

- What spiritual belief are you holding onto out of habit rather than alignment?

- When have you felt the freedom to explore or question your faith journey?

- What would you try as an experiment if you called "New Choice" on your current belief system?

Script Revision:

Every rehearsal ends with a new line to carry forward. Try this one on and let it guide your next decision:

> *"I trust my path, even when it doesn't look like anyone else's. I am allowed to explore, evolve, and choose again."*

Encore: The Faith to Choose Again

Belief is a living manuscript, scribbled in pencil, coffee-stained with doubt, and sometimes rewritten from a blank page. We're born into a worldview, shaped by family, culture, and circumstance, but life invites us to question it. We experience loss, love, learning, and renewal. Through it all, faith keeps evolving, sometimes quietly, sometimes in leaps of courage.

Maybe that's what faith really is. Not blind devotion. Not rigid rules. Just the willingness to stay in the conversation. To keep listening. To keep evolving.

For me, spirituality has never been about having all the answers. My faith has been about staying curious enough to keep asking better questions.

Improv gave me the language for what my spirit already knew: when something no longer works, you don't force it. You call "New Choice" because new choices bring freedom, wisdom, and courage.

You have space to believe something new. To mix tradition with rebellion. To let go of what no longer fits and reach for something that does. Faith can change shape. It can soften, sharpen, quiet down, or rise in your own voice. You do not need permission. You already have it.

Walk into a sanctuary. Sit under a tree. Stare up at the stars. Or hold a quiet space for whatever is sacred to you. You are allowed to seek. You are allowed to shift. You are allowed to start again. You are allowed to improvise.

Script Notes: Rewriting My Faith Story

These are the moments that reshaped how I connect to something greater, whether through religion, community, curiosity, or improv. Use them as inspiration to find your own New Choice moments on your spiritual path.

1. Choosing Catholicism at Nine Years Old

Instead of blindly following, I explored. At age nine, I visited my mother's church, sat through four hours of Seventh-day Adventist services, and decided that it wasn't for me. The choice gave me my first taste of spiritual agency.

2. Walking Away from the Church

When a priest refused to help me during one of the darkest seasons of my life, I didn't just lose trust in him. I lost trust in the institution. The choice to walk away was about protecting my spirit, and not about giving up.

3. Getting Baptized Again

Years later, after rediscovering Christianity through non-denominational churches, I made a New Choice. I got baptized again, as a born-again Christian. My new choice allowed me to reclaim my relationship with God.

4. Leaving a Marriage That Didn't Reflect My Faith

I once believed that being a "biblical wife" meant staying in a bad marriage, no matter what. When a coach asked, "Would Christ want His daughter to be this unhappy?" something shifted. My new choice helped me see that faith and freedom aren't opposites.

5. Naming Religion as a Non-Negotiable While Dating

When my now-husband asked me out for a Sunday, I said, "I'm going to church." That was my test. His reply of "Can I come with you?" spoke volumes. My new choice opened the door to a shared spiritual journey.

6. Letting Improv Be Sacred

I stopped compartmentalizing. I started seeing improv as part of my faith practice: a space of inclusion, grace, and listening. My new choice transformed a stage into a sanctuary.

Chapter 14

Choosing Time To Succeed

Clarifying What Matters Before You Fill the Calendar

"Time is the coin of your life. It is the only coin you have, and only you can determine how it will be spent. Be careful lest you let other people spend it for you." — Carl Sandburg

I'm on a deadline to finish this book but I never planned to write a chapter about choosing how you spend your time until I realized how much pivoting I do by the minute with my schedule.

As I write this chapter, I'm moments away from starting graduate school. Suddenly, I have found the time to complete this project that you are experiencing.

The number one complaint I hear from most people, at all professional levels is: *"I don't have enough time."*

Let's be real: none of us is short on time. We all have the same 24 hours in a day, 168 hours in a week, and 8,760 hours in a year. The real issue is how we choose to spend those hours. Saying "I don't have time" is usually code for "I didn't prioritize this" or "I didn't manage myself effectively." That is an easy excuse, one I've used plenty of times myself.

Time management is self-management. Yet, most people are managing nothing at all. In fact, 82% of people don't use a structured system to manage their time. They rely on their inbox, to-do lists, or chaos to dictate the day. No wonder 89% of employees waste time daily, and 75.5% of students regularly procrastinate.

My First Lessons in Time

My first real lesson in managing myself around time came from flea markets. As a kid, I worked at them with my dad, Carmie. He was the driver, so I didn't have a choice about what time we left the house. If I wasn't ready, I got left behind.

What stuck with me most wasn't the early wake-ups; it was Carmie's mantra: "Always be an hour early." At the time, I thought it was overkill. Honestly, I still do. But over the years, I saw what that mindset created: calm, preparation, and a sense of respect for time, for others, and for myself.

Being early gave me breathing room. In college, that structure saved me. Between classes, internships, jobs, and late-night improv shows, I didn't have time to waste. I had to be strategic. I learned to prioritize, rank competing demands, and map out what was doable in a week. That ability gave me a quiet kind of confidence. I could say yes to opportunities without drowning.

More importantly, I learned when to say no.

Relearning What I Already Knew

Years later, when I got accepted into grad school while working full-time and writing this book, I panicked. Could I really do it all?

For a moment, I doubted myself, until I remembered that in undergrad, I once took five classes, held a full-time job, and interned. I already had the skills. I just needed to reactivate them.

Not everyone gets that kind of early training. The more I coach, the more I see how many people operate without any system at all. They're not lacking hours; they're lacking structure.

The Psychology of Time

There's a concept called Parkinson's Law: "Work expands to fill the time allotted for its completion." Translation: the more time you give yourself, the longer it tends to take.

If you've ever wrapped up a major project the night before vacation, you know the flip side of this law is also true. That last-minute adrenaline rush? That's what I call the "vacation effect."

Attorney and business strategist Denise Gosnell, who was a guest on my podcast, even wrote a book on it *(The Vacation Effect)*. The idea is simple: when the clock tightens, your mindset sharpens.

Cultural Clocks and Time Norms

When I moved to the Southern U.S., I learned that time can also be cultural. I once scheduled a meeting for 3:00 p.m. and was told kindly to expect people between 3 and 3:30 p.m.

At first, I was thrown off. I'd come from environments where punctuality was a form of professionalism. I learned to adapt and clarified how I wanted to operate within different time cultures. We all come from different rhythms. Understanding both your own and others' is key.

Time Thieves: What Drains You

As my schedule became more complex, I began to notice the things that drained my time and energy without giving anything in return. I call them time thieves.

Time thieves are distractions that add up fast: Meetings that didn't need to happen, "quick" favors that derail your day, guilt-driven yeses, doom-scrolling, mindless multitasking, over-volunteering.

Sometimes, these distractions appear to be productivity, but they actually rob you of focus and hijack your priorities.

For me, one of the biggest thieves was people-pleasing. Improv trained me to say "yes, and…" by default, which became a problem when I kept saying yes to things I didn't want to do or have time for. Eventually, all those yeses added up to burnout.

Boundaries Are the Real Issue

We don't just lose time. We give it away. We let our schedules get filled by default. We prioritize other people's urgencies over our own. Then we wonder why we're exhausted.

If you want to write a book, change careers, or heal your health, you must protect the time it takes. You can't wait for time to open up. You must carve it out, block it, and guard it. More importantly, in my opinion, you have to be honest about what's getting in the way.

Outcome Goals vs. Process Goals

One major mistake people make is focusing on outcomes like: "Write the book," or "Get in shape." By "mistake", I mean we declare a giant and overwhelming outcome goal without a plan. If these goals are not scheduled, they may not happen.

Process goals are the small, bite-sized steps that move you and your outcome goals forward. Scheduling "write one chapter" of the book each week has a higher probability of coming to fruition than scheduling "write a book" on my calendar. For me, it meant setting aside time to outline, write 1,000 words, edit, or conduct research. Once I gave those actions space on the calendar, momentum kicked in. I schedule every aspect of my life, which seems counterintuitive with my improv nature.

Some days, I feel like I'm living a double life, one part structure, one part improv. Knowing how to leverage both skill sets is the perfect recipe, as I don't panic when things don't go as planned or according to schedule. I simply pivot and reschedule.

Structure Creates Sanity

One of the best tools I apply, as well as teach others, is the popular Eisenhower Matrix, which breaks tasks into four quadrants:

1. Urgent and Important: Do it now.

2. Important but Not Urgent: Schedule it.

3. Urgent but Not Important: Delegate it.

4. Not Urgent or Important: Eliminate it.

Categorizing your tasks makes your choices visible and your time intentional. Prioritize the urgent and important because those are the activities that elevate your goals, especially if only you have the expertise to complete specific tasks. For example, only I can write my point of view in this book, but I'm relying on editors to do the rest because it's not a strong quality for me.

Even the best time strategy won't shield you from real life. Emergencies happen. Grief happens. Plans fall apart. I've had perfectly structured weeks implode overnight.

What saves me on most days is my own flexibility, plus having room or contingency. When I mentioned that I schedule everything, I mean everything, including time for handling last-minute urgencies and emergencies. On my calendar, you will find "buffer zones", sometimes labeled as "Transition" and "Prep". I no longer rush from meeting to meeting or activity to activity without any scheduled downtime. My approach to my calendar in this way is what I call "time banking." I basically set aside windows of time that look like I'm busy so I can be my own time thief. Yes, I reclaim my time if I need to, allowing for a busy yet calm day.

The Hidden Cost of "No Time"

Busy has become a badge of honor, but busyness isn't productivity. Behind most time struggles is a lack of structure, not a lack of hours.

People react to time, not manage it. Stressed-out reactions lead to burnout, procrastination, and overwhelm. This reality affects everyone, including professionals, entrepreneurs, parents, children, and students. What starts as a calendar problem becomes a quality-of-life issue.

I call it time poverty: the chronic sense that no matter how hard you work, it's never enough, which leads to rushed decisions, missed opportunities, and exhaustion disguised as effort.

Intentional Constraints Create Freedom

Parkinson's Law has a flip side: focus expands when time contracts, which is why deadlines matter. Constraints sharpen clarity.

Parkinson's Corollary goes further: work consumes all available resources unless you set limits. Limitations don't just create urgency; they create efficiency.

The Data Behind the Drama

In the fast-moving reality of business, I've seen improv-inspired time habits create results you can measure. Teams that once spun their wheels in indecision started finishing projects faster by ditching perfection in favor of forward motion. When they stopped chasing perfection and started taking the next best step, momentum took over.

Meetings shrank, decision-making accelerated, and the energy in the room shifted from frazzled to focused. With a little structure and a lot of presence, conversations became clearer, faster, and more productive.

Morale followed. Teams began operating with less panic and more trust. They learned to adapt instead of reacting. They didn't just manage time better. They changed the way they worked inside it.

Culture shifts when people stop drowning in details and start making choices that reflect their priorities. Improv gave them the tools, and time discipline made those tools stick.

Improv and the Art of Timing

Improv might be one of the most powerful tools for learning timing, not just on stage but in life.

In comedy, timing is everything. Deliver a punchline too early or too late, and the laugh falls flat, but it's not just about humor. Persuasion, storytelling, leadership, and connection all rely on timing. The only way to develop great timing is through one foundational skill: presence or being present.

Improv sharpens your ability to listen with your ears, and also with your eyes, your body, and your intuition. The more present you are, the more you can sense the right moment to speak, pause, respond, pivot, or hold space. Of all my stagecraft skills I've learned in improv, this one is the most powerful because presence is a life skill we all need.

One of the first things I teach new improvisers is to *"get the important information out early in a scene"* because it creates clarity, structure, and trust between scene partners. The same goes for life: when you start something without clear information, it creates ambiguity. Ambiguity breeds stress. On stage, we only have a few minutes to build a whole world, which means we don't have time to meander or withhold. We must make bold choices, quickly and clearly.

I call this functional timing: making choices that support collaboration, reduce stress, and keep momentum alive.

Improv also teaches the importance of brevity. When performers dump too much information at once, it overwhelms both the audience and their scene partner, leading to brain overload, also known as cognitive overload. People disengage. The same thing happens in meetings, emails, and everyday conversations. Timing isn't just about when you say something; it's also about how much you say and how clearly you deliver it. The brain is lazy and looks for short cuts. Less is more.

Timing, Awareness, and Flow

Contrary to popular belief, improv doesn't just make you faster. Trained improvisers may appear quick on their feet, and this is because they are hyper-aware of themselves and others in the moment. Self-awareness is key to managing time well because sometimes, we lose track of time for good reason: we're in a state of flow. Flow is beautiful because it's where creativity resides.

While writing this book, I've been able to get into that flow state, but only if I've created the space for it. For me, that means blocking entire days to immerse myself in the process. I've tried all the methods: writing at 5 a.m., sprint sessions, Pomodoro timers. They all have their place, but for certain creative projects, too much constraint kills momentum, and there is research to support this.

A NASA study proved that rigid time blocks can inhibit creativity, especially for adults. Most of us were trained in school to compartmentalize our time: math for 50 minutes, reading for 50 minutes, and so on, and we learned to suppress our creative instincts in favor of efficiency.

Creativity doesn't work like that. Creativity needs space, flexibility, and improvisation. Timing creativity produces mediocrity, in my opinion.

Structured Freedom: The Improv Paradox

Improv is the sweet spot between structure and freedom. On stage, we operate with tight constraints: limited time, no script, and high stakes. Yet within those constraints, we find ways to adapt, build, and collaborate because we stay present, listen, and trust ourselves to make the next right choice.

In life, we face similar tensions. Schedules. Deadlines. Limited energy. But when we bring an improviser's mindset to those challenges, we start to use time more intentionally. We speak with clarity. We show up with presence. We stop overloading our calendars with noise and start listening for what really matters.

Ways To Choose Your Time With Intention

Structured freedom sounds like a contradiction, but in practice, it's where power lives. A well-built calendar with room to pivot becomes more than a schedule; it becomes a support system. Once you stop reacting and start designing your days, momentum builds. The next move is about making conscious, aligned choices. The following tools will help you do just that so that you can reclaim time and direct it where it matters most.

Scene Work:

Take the stage and move from theory to practice with these quick drills to help you catch your defaults, pivot in the moment, and train your brain for change.

- Conduct a Time Audit: Track how you spend your time for three consecutive days. Highlight anything that felt like a "should" rather than a "want" or left you drained with little to show.

- Define Outcome and Process Goals: Choose one meaningful goal and break it into specific, time-blockable process steps. Schedule these like appointments rather than trying to "fit them in."

- Practice "Not Right Now": Before saying yes to requests this week, ask: "Is this aligned with my goals? Is this the best use of my energy? Is this a time thief in disguise?"

Side Coaching:

Before making more choices, pause and check in. The following prompts will help you be honest about what's on autopilot and what needs to change.

- What does "I don't have time" mean when you say it?

- Where are you over-giving your time out of guilt, fear, or habit?

- What would change if you protected your time as carefully as you protect others?

Script Revision:

Every rehearsal ends with a new line to carry forward. Try this one on and let it guide your next decision:

"I don't manage time; I manage my choices. Every hour reflects what I value, and I choose with intention."

Encore: Make a New Choice with Your Time

No one really plans the moment that changes everything. This chapter wasn't on my original outline, but it kept nudging me in coaching sessions, late-night reflections, and hallway conversations where people admitted they were drowning in their schedules. Not because they were lazy. Not because they lacked goals. They just didn't feel like they had control.

Time isn't the villain in your story. You already have enough of it to change your life. The challenge is deciding who gets it, what earns it, and how to stop handing it out like candy at a parade. That means setting boundaries and designing your days with care, not stuffing them with obligations.

Many people unknowingly give away their time. They say yes out of habit or guilt. They get caught in the swirl of urgency and mistake it for meaning. They end up exhausted and overextended, unable to recall how they got there.

Here's your moment to take the lead.

Choose to stop apologizing for protecting your energy. Choose to build a structure that breathes, not cages. Choose to stop confusing busy with valuable. Make space on your calendar for the things that fuel you. Choose to make decisions with clarity, not just convenience.

The clock is not the problem. What matters is how you show up for it. Every hour you spend is a vote for the life you want. You don't need permission to claim it. Time isn't running out. Make a new choice, even if it's not on the schedule!

Script Notes: Reclaiming My Time

Use these moments as reminders that your time belongs to you. One bold boundary, one intentional "no," one restructured calendar can change everything.

1. Leaving the House an Hour Early (Because Dad Said So)

As a kid, my dad drilled into me that being early was non-negotiable. At the time, I rolled my eyes. Now? That buffer zone is my sanity saver, and the first boundary I ever learned to protect.

2. Balancing Five College Classes with Two Jobs and Improv

I didn't just survive a packed schedule. I mastered it. That stretch taught me how to prioritize fast, recover from overwhelm, and prove to myself what I was capable of handling.

3. Saying No to the "Quick" Favor That Wrecked My Week

The request seemed small. Just a quick yes, but that one favor spiraled my whole calendar. Losing time for others' agendas taught me how fast people-pleasing turns into time theft, and how good it feels to protect your peace.

4. Creating Space for Disruption

Instead of pretending life would go perfectly, I started building blank space into my calendar, because things will go sideways. When they do, I don't spiral. I pivot.

5. Turning Off Notifications to Turn On My Brain

I silenced the pings, dings, and constant pull of other people's urgency. Making that small shift gave me hours back and made me realize how much of my time was being spent on things that weren't even mine.

6. Blocking Time for a Book I Was "Too Busy" to Write

Writing this book sat on my goal list for years. The shift didn't happen when I found the time. I made time to make it happen. Scheduling it was the moment I stopped treating my goals like optional extras.

Chapter 15
Choosing to Pursue Purpose & Passion Over Pressure

"The meaning of life is to find your gift. The purpose of life is to give it away." — Pablo Picasso

I've wrestled with the words 'passion' and 'purpose' when it comes to what drives you. Sometimes, passion becomes purpose, and sometimes, purpose evolves into passion.

Even saying that brings a sense of déjà vu. Maybe I've said it before, heard it somewhere, or was coached through it. I've gone in circles over which word matters more. I even considered writing two separate chapters. I see purpose and passion as two separate gloves. Each is meaningful on its own, but they're only truly powerful when paired together.

Purpose remains one of the most powerful motivators in both work and life. People want to know they matter. Their time, talent, and energy should contribute to something meaningful. A sense of connection to a larger vision drives deeper engagement.

According to research published by the American Psychological Association, individuals with a strong sense of purpose tend to report higher levels of optimism, resilience, and life satisfaction. They're more likely to make healthy choices, recover faster from stress, and maintain emotional well-being during difficult seasons. Purpose lifts you up and doesn't just keep you going.

Passion, on the other hand, sparks the fire. When you're passionate about your work, it doesn't feel like work, and when you're working in your purpose, that passion deepens.

In business, the pattern holds true as well. Leaders who recognize the human desire to contribute see stronger performance, higher morale, and better cultures. Employees want more than a paycheck. Purpose motivates them. When they feel seen and valued, retention improves, effort increases, and commitment grows.

Passion and purpose work best together. Both matter. My love for improv performance evolved into a purpose that impacts people. My desire to help others build better relationships is rooted in purpose. The joy I find in watching people grow through training started as a passion and became my mission.

The two forces of passion and purpose are collaborative, not competitive.

Before I take you into the stories that shaped my understanding of purpose and passion, let's get clear on what these words really mean because they're not just buzzwords. They're two very different forces, and understanding how they work can shape every decision ahead.

Defining the Difference: Passion vs. Purpose

People often use the words purpose and passion interchangeably, but they're not the same thing. I've spent years wrestling with these two concepts, trying to define them, live them, and at times, choose between them. You don't have to choose, but you need to understand how they're different and work together.

Passion fuels the fire. Time disappears when you're fully in it. Emotion drives the energy. Urgency adds momentum. Obsession sometimes takes over. Passion stays personal. No paycheck or spotlight is needed. You feel it in your bones when the work feels right. Performing, designing, coaching, creating, fixing, and building all flow with ease.

Purpose pulls you forward. The reason behind the effort becomes your why. Feelings take a back seat to impact. Purpose lives in contribution, service, and legacy. It keeps you showing up on the hard days, even when the spark goes missing. Curveballs land, and purpose holds the ground beneath you. Passion loves the doing. Purpose values the outcome.

Passion often arrives first. The spark grabs your attention and pulls you in. Purpose keeps you going. You might feel passionate about acting or speaking, but the moment your words help someone change their life, something shifts. Passion begins the journey. Purpose gives it meaning.

This distinction became even clearer when I discovered Simon Sinek's *Start With Why* framework. Sinek's theory explains that every individual and organization operates on three levels: **What** they do, **How** they do it, and **Why** they do it. Most people can articulate the first two, their products, their methods, but very few can define their why, the deeper belief that drives their actions. The why represents purpose, cause, or belief. It's the reason you get out of bed in the morning and the reason anyone should care.

According to Sinek, true inspiration happens from the inside out. Passion may ignite action, but purpose sustains it. Passion lives in the what, the craft, the excitement, the emotional charge of creation. Purpose lives in the why, the contribution that gives meaning to all of it. When we start with why, we move from chasing excitement to living alignment.

Passion and purpose don't always move in sync. Passion can evolve. Purpose can deepen. Sometimes they shift. Sometimes they collide. Passion brings excitement. Purpose brings fulfillment. One sparks the fire. The other keeps it burning.

Chasing only passion leads to burnout. Following only purpose, without emotional connection, can feel heavy and draining. Both are essential. When passion and purpose align, everything clicks. You love what you do, and it matters. You feel alive and grounded. Others feel it too because the light in you shines outward.

Every day offers opportunities to live at the intersection of passion and purpose, while helping others discover that same powerful alignment.

From Childhood Dreams to Couple's Work

The Engineer and the Entertainer

Some people know their purpose from an early age. My stepson is one of them. From the time he was young, he knew he wanted to be an engineer. He set his sights on it, built a path, and stuck with it. As I write this book, he's about to head off to Purdue University to study engineering.

That's a crystal-clear purpose in motion.

Mine was different, but just as strong. I also knew what I wanted early on. At age seven, I told my mom I wanted to be an actress. I'd been watching The Dinah Shore Show in the 1970s, and I imagined myself being interviewed on that show. I don't know why I wanted it. I just knew.

When I told my mom, she laughed and said, "You can't do that." Her reaction only made me want it more.

While I didn't become a traditional Hollywood actress, I did become a performer, in every sense of the word. Whether I'm speaking onstage at a corporate sales conference or performing improv in a comedy club, I'm doing what I set out to do.

Building a Team and Finding My Calling

Later in life, another shift took hold. After moving to a new city, I started hiring and training a new team. What surprised me most was how many people had never received even the most basic customer service training.

I brought in an improv-based training company to work with them. The company resembled the one I now lead. As I watched my team move through the experience, something changed. The energy in the room lifted. People leaned in. Walls came down. The training wasn't just helpful; it was transformational.

Bob Burg teaches in *The Go-Giver* that "your influence is determined by how abundantly you place other people's interests first." Watching my team learn to make each other look good through improv was that principle in action. Burg's philosophy challenges the scarcity mindset that often dominates corporate culture, the idea that success must be competitive or self-protective. Instead, it reframes influence as generosity. When we focus on serving others and creating value, we build trust, collaboration, and genuine connection. Improv works the same way. "Yes, And" requires participants to listen with intent, accept ideas with openness, and respond with support. Each choice reinforces the success of the whole group rather than individual ego.

Similarly, Patrick Lencioni, in *The Five Dysfunctions of a Team*, identifies trust as the foundation of all team effectiveness. Without trust, people protect themselves instead of the mission. They hold back ideas, avoid conflict, and disengage emotionally. What I unknowingly witnessed during that improv training session was Lencioni's model in fast-forward: vulnerability-based trust building in real time. When team members risk being silly, imperfect, or wrong, and are met with laughter, acceptance, and encouragement, they experience psychological safety firsthand.

The walls of self-preservation fall away. What's left is connection, courage, and belonging.

When people practice "Yes, And" together, they aren't just improvising; they're rehearsing the principles of high-performing teams. They learn to listen to understand, not to reply. They build on each other's ideas instead of competing for airtime. They replace fear of failure with shared momentum. In that space, Burg's generosity and Lencioni's trust converge, creating the cultural foundation every thriving organization needs.

Watching that session with my team unfold sparked something in me. Passion met purpose in a new way. I didn't want to manage people. I wanted to equip them. I wanted to build healthy, high-performing teams where people felt confident, supported, and connected,teams that created more than good service. Teams that created joy. Fulfilled employees serve better. Customers feel the difference.

Purpose came into focus. I wanted to give people tools, knowledge, and confidence to grow. I wanted to shape environments where people felt empowered to show up fully. Culture shifts when people feel that. Leadership strengthens. Results improve. Impact lasts.

According to research from Cigna and McKinsey, organizations that foster purpose-driven environments see up to 40 percent higher employee retention and significantly greater engagement. Results like that reflect something deeper. People stay and perform when they know they matter.

One training experience changed everything. It led to the company I run today. It shaped the mission I live every day.

A Shared Purpose, A New Chapter

A new purpose continues to take shape. Personal and spiritual layers run deep. The message stirred during a church sermon and revealed itself as a calling: partner with my husband to help other couples.

Our lived experiences created the foundation. Past relationships, divorce, healing, and growth shaped us into guides. Some couples are rebuilding. Some individuals are healing after heartbreak. Others are searching for real connection. A strong pull keeps leading me to this work.

We carry the purpose together. The passion behind it strengthens the mission. When purpose and passion align in service to others, the work becomes sacred.

Just as purpose shifted in my work, it began expanding in other areas of my life too. The research only deepened that understanding.

What the Research Reveals About Purpose and Passion

People use the phrase "find your purpose" as if it were simple, as if one day you would wake up with your mission fully formed, your path laid out, and your passion instantly ready to monetize.

Reality looks different. Most people wrestle with purpose. That struggle isn't weakness. It's human.

Researchers define purpose as a long-term intention to accomplish something meaningful that reaches beyond the self. It goes deeper than goals. Purpose shows up when values, identity, and contribution align in a clear and meaningful way. It becomes the fuel behind your why. It carries you through dry spells and adds weight to both the wins and the chaos.

Purpose Isn't Just a Feeling. Purpose Is a Force.

People don't pursue a purpose to decorate a vision board. They pursue it because it gives them something to live for, especially during the hard seasons.

Those with a strong sense of purpose tend to feel more hopeful, resilient, and satisfied. One major study found a 46 percent lower risk of death among individuals with a high purpose. Another revealed a 43 percent reduction in depression, along with better emotional well-being and less loneliness.

Purposeful people do more than dream. They take better care of themselves, recover faster, seek growth, and stay connected.

The benefits grow stronger with age. Purpose has been linked to lower rates of cognitive decline, stronger memory, and even a reduced risk of Alzheimer's. Staying connected to meaning matters more than staying busy. Purpose doesn't just keep people alive. It keeps them engaged in life.

Why So Many People Still Feel Lost

Only 25 percent of young people report having a clear sense of purpose. The majority are still searching and unsure where to begin.

That statistic stopped me in my tracks. My stepson came to mind right away. From an early age, he knew he wanted to be an engineer and built his life around that goal. Most people don't operate with that level of clarity. Most need time to explore, question, and experiment before finding a right path.

Culture often glorifies certainty and productivity. Uncertainty gets mislabeled as failure. By adulthood, people are expected to have everything figured out. When they don't, shame creeps in. Silence follows. That pressure traps people in roles or routines that no longer fit. Pivoting feels risky. Not having a clear answer feels like a weakness.

Passion: The Spark That Keeps You Moving

Purpose answers the "why." Passion fuels the "what." Passion pulls you in with spark, energy, and a feeling of aliveness that refuses to be ignored.

People who regularly engage in meaningful activities report 34 percent less stress and 18 percent less sadness. Passion brings vitality and presence. Flow follows when focus sharpens and time loses its grip.

Challenges feel different when passion is involved. Passionate people keep moving. Creativity expands. Persistence grows. Resourcefulness emerges. Commitment rises from a deep sense of care.

Passion can also carry complexity. Fading interest, shifting desires, or the weight of expectation often get mistaken for passion. Chasing what seems impressive can silence what feels true.

Misaligned effort drains energy and opens the door to burnout.

Harmonious passion offers a healthier path. Researchers describe it as the kind that blends into life without overtaking it. Energy increases, but space remains for everything else that matters.

The Sweet Spot: When Passion Meets Purpose

What happens when passion and purpose finally align? The results speak for themselves.

Researcher Morten Hansen studied thousands of professionals and found that those who combined passion and purpose performed at the 80th percentile. Those with purpose alone ranked in the 64th percentile. Those with only passion dropped to the 20th. The data confirmed what I've witnessed in coaching and business. Passion gets people in the game. Purpose keeps them playing and performing at their best.

Business reflects the same truth. When employees believe their work matters, everything shifts. Engagement rises. Loyalty deepens. Resilience strengthens. The same joint study by McKinsey and Cigna that I referenced earlier also found that purpose-driven employees are healthier, more productive, and more likely to become stronger ambassadors for the company.

Purpose builds people. Purpose builds culture.

Motivation plays a role, too. When I introduced improv to my team, I expected skill development. What I witnessed was a complete energy shift. Confidence grew. Morale lifted. Connection deepened. Data from TeamStage and the Motivational Speakers Agency supports this. Motivated employees are 87 percent less likely to resign and show a 20 percent increase in performance. The training was effective, but the real success came from creating an environment where people felt part of something bigger.

When passion and purpose work together, the experience changes. People stop clocking in and start building, contributing, and growing. They show up with heart and move things forward.

I've lived that alignment. Performance alone gave me passion, but not always impact. Mission-driven work gave me purpose but often left me tired. Both came alive when I started using improv to teach, coach, and connect. Passion gave me energy. Purpose gave me focus.

Together, they gave me staying power. The tool that turned purpose and passion into action was improv.

Improv offered more than a performance style. It became a framework for leading, coaching, connecting, and shaping culture. Each exercise revealed a more profound lesson. Listening, adapting, trusting, and creating moved beyond the stage. They became essential life skills.

In every business setting where I applied improv, the impact became clear. Communication improved. Confidence increased. Teams grew stronger, more connected, and more engaged. A clear realization followed. Improv had nothing to do with being funny. It had everything to do with being present.

What Improv Teaches Us About Passion and Purpose

Improv began as a creative outlet. I wanted to perform, to entertain, to challenge myself on stage. What started as stage practice quickly turned into life practice.

One of the first lessons was to say yes to what's real. In improv scenes, you learn to accept the offer in front of you and build from it. I began doing the same in life. Instead of resisting uncertainty or waiting for perfect timing, I started paying attention to what pulled me forward. Curiosity became more important than clarity.

Listening became an anchor. Improv helped me focus with more intention, both on others and on myself. I started paying attention to how my body responded in different moments. Some experiences brought energy, while others created a sense of heaviness. The contrast revealed patterns. A loud calling never arrived. Subtle cues had been speaking all along. I finally started listening.

Overthinking lost its grip once I began trusting small instincts. In improv, you move before you plan. That practice spilled over into my choices. Certainty stopped being the requirement. A flicker of interest became enough to explore the next step. Some of the most meaningful work in my life began with a hunch.

The concept of new choice shaped me more than any script ever could. In every improv class, that phrase meant freedom. If a scene stalled, we didn't cling. We shifted. I started applying that idea everywhere. When my goals no longer aligned with who I had become, I allowed myself to move on. Choosing again didn't feel like quitting. It felt like evolving.

Improv also reminded me that growth rarely happens alone. Collaboration is baked into every scene. I stopped treating purpose as something I had to figure out in isolation. Support became part of the process. People showed up when I let them in.

Curiosity kept returning. I followed what felt alive rather than waiting for guarantees. Each step led to another. Action replaced analysis.

Over time, improv evolved into more than just a tool. The practice helped me reconnect with what matters most. Listening, trusting, adjusting, and responding created a framework I could carry into every part of life. The focus shifted away from performance. The work began to center around purpose.

Feeling stuck can take many forms. You might feel torn between what you love and what you feel called to do. You might feel unsure of your direction or disconnected from what once mattered. Wherever you find yourself, improv offers a way forward.

Improv scenes often lose momentum. Strong performers don't force or fix. They respond with two simple words: new choice.

The power in that phrase comes from what it releases. Nothing needs to be broken to call for change. Sometimes momentum fades. Sometimes alignment slips. No shame. No apology. Just movement. A clear decision, made with curiosity over control.

Apply the same mindset offstage.

A job that drains you? Make a new choice.

A project that no longer excites you? Make a new choice.

A plan that once made sense but now feels limiting? Make a new choice. A story you've outgrown? Make a new choice.

You don't need a perfect plan. You need a pattern of movement. Purpose and passion respond to momentum. Begin by showing up. Listen more closely. Try something small. Choose again.

Growth begins when you stop forcing the old script and respond to what feels true in the present moment.

Say it out loud: New choice.
Name the moment that needs it.
Then move forward.

Improv Your Way into Purpose and Passion

You don't need all the answers to start. You just need a willingness to listen, choose, and shift when it's time.

Try these exercises to move from overthinking to intentional action.

Scene Work:

Take the stage and move from theory to practice with these quick drills to help you catch your defaults, pivot in the moment, and train your brain for change.

- Say "Yes, And" to Where You Are: Write about one truth you've resisted about your current situation. Create a "Yes, And" statement that accepts where you are while building forward.

- Trust Your First Instinct: Identify one idea or calling that keeps surfacing for you. Take one small action this week without overthinking. Make the call, sign up, or start exploring.

- Three-Day Curiosity Challenge: Do something you've never done for three consecutive days. Journal what you discover about yourself and look for patterns that energize you.

Side Coaching:

Before making more choices, pause and check in. The following prompts will help you be honest about what's on autopilot and what needs to change.

- Where are you currently feeling stuck or unfulfilled?

- When was the last time you felt truly on purpose and alive?

- What part of your current story are you ready to rewrite?

Script Revision:

Every rehearsal ends with a new line to carry forward. Try this one on and let it guide your next decision:

"I am not stuck. I am improvising with purpose. Every choice is a chance to grow and discover what excites me."

Encore: Purpose That Stays, Passion That Moves

Passion grabs your heart. Purpose grounds your steps.

One brings the spark, and the other brings direction. When they sync, your next step feels clearer and more energizing.

Improv taught me that alignment doesn't require a perfect plan. It asks for something simpler: presence, curiosity, and the courage to choose again.

You don't need all the answers to begin. You need a willingness to follow what lights you up and let meaning emerge along the way.

When the script stops working, rewrite it. When you feel stuck, find what still feels alive. Start there.

Purpose and passion aren't destinations. They force you to engage with daily. Action creates alignment.

One moment. One choice. That's where momentum begins. Start there. Choose again.

Script Notes: Reclaiming My Purpose & Passion

Use these moments as reminders that you're allowed to evolve. One pivot, one pause, one bold decision can reignite everything.

1. Watching an Improv Company Train My Staff

I didn't expect a corporate training session to change my life, but it did. On that day, I realized my passion was helping people grow.

2. Choosing a Stage Over a Desk

Even when it didn't make sense on paper, I kept choosing the microphone, the spotlight, the story. Those choices weren't detours. They were direction.

3. Turning Marriage Lessons into a Mission

What my husband and I experienced was purposeful. Our shared experience became a calling to help others heal and reconnect.

4. Letting Passion and Purpose Trade Places

Sometimes, I chased what I loved, and sometimes, I showed up for what mattered. The magic happened when I stopped trying to force a label and just followed what felt right.

5. Saying "New Choice" When the Old One No Longer Fit

I've walked away from paths that looked good on the outside but didn't feel true on the inside.

Chapter 16
Choosing A Peaceful Ending

Embracing The Final Scene

"Death ends a life, not a relationship." — Mitch Albom, Tuesdays with Morrie

Death didn't belong in the original plan for this book. The topic felt too heavy, too personal, and too easy to avoid until one ordinary coffee meeting made it impossible to ignore.

I was talking to my business coach, who also happens to be my spiritual guide. The conversation started with a question that had been haunting me: Should I euthanize my 18-year-old Shih Tzu, Roxy? I didn't want to play God, but I also didn't want her to suffer. As I spoke through my uncertainty, he shared that he had been caring for his terminally ill uncle. That opened a door neither of us expected. The conversation spiraled into real talk about death, grief, logistics, dignity, and all the ways we try to control the uncontrollable.

We kept going. Like in improv, one topic led to the next: end-of-life planning, delayed grief, and family dynamics. These are the parts of death people rarely discuss, even though they affect us all.

Most people believe those conversations matter. A recent study found that 90% of Americans believe discussing end-of-life care is essential, yet only 27% have actually done so. Fewer than half have a will. Among people under 35, that number drops closer to 20. We know death is coming, but we rarely prepare for it. We push it off as if it's an optional part of life.

That mindset is evident everywhere, including in the popular "life wheel" often used in life coaching, which breaks down life into tidy categories, such as health, relationships, finances, and career. Death never makes the list, even though it impacts every category. We lose people we love. We grieve parts of ourselves. We plan for the inevitable or leave it for someone else to manage.

This chapter is a New Choice: a choice to stop skipping the hard stuff, to tell the truth about grief, and to treat death not as a detour but as part of the road.

Improv taught me how to keep going when the script falls apart. When nothing is certain, attention becomes the only thing we can truly offer. Death demands that same level of presence. It strips away the illusion of control and asks us to show up anyway.

No one gets out of this life untouched by death. What matters is how we respond. With presence. With preparation. With love. That's the choice we get to make.

My First Real Loss

I didn't expect my father to die when he did. He had been sick for most of my life, with congestive heart failure beginning when I was still a kid. By my senior year of high school, his illness had lasted more than a decade. Somewhere in me, the awareness lived quietly. The day would come. I just didn't know how to face it.

My Catholic high school offered a class called Death and Dying, based on the book of the same title by Elisabeth Kubler-Ross. I signed up. At the time, studying death felt safer than facing it. I mistakenly assumed academic preparation equaled emotional readiness.

No one tells you how hard it will hit. Grief keeps its own clock. No amount of preparation can change when it strikes or how long it lasts. When it lands, it steals your breath and leaves you stunned.

I was 22, just two weeks into my first real job after college, still trying to prove I belonged. That night, my mom called and invited me to dinner. My dad wanted to see me. I told her I couldn't. I stayed late to impress my boss.

Later that evening, I came home from work and took a shower. The phone rang. The answering machine picked up. I could hear my mother's tearful voice through the sound of streaming water: "Your father's in the hospital again, and I think you should come this time."

My stomach dropped. He had been in and out of the hospital so many times that I had started treating it like a routine. He had bounced back so many times; I convinced myself he always would.

He didn't.

We arrived at the hospital and were sent to a private family room. Nothing good ever follows that kind of separation. When the doctor entered, I already knew. He told us my father was gone. My body stayed upright, but everything inside collapsed.

I asked to see him. I needed it to be real. The staff allowed me in. I remember the cold steel of the table, the stillness of his face, the rigor mortis throughout his body, the way time stopped inside that room. My brother eventually had to pull me out.

The next few days blurred together: funeral planning, family tension, calls to my half-sister in Connecticut, and trying to keep my mother upright while keeping myself from falling apart. My brother-in-law and I went to the funeral home. The director launched into his pitch like we were shopping for a used car.

"This one's waterproof," he said.

"Waterproof?" I stared at him. "He's not going swimming."

He wouldn't have cared. I asked for a wooden box. Simple, honest, and the way my father would have wanted it.

Tension showed up anyway. Relatives who hadn't spoken to him in years appeared at the funeral. A few even asked for his things. I didn't have the time or energy to be shocked. I was the one handling the logistics. Death certificates. Insurance claims. Financial paperwork. My mother couldn't carry any of it.

Just a few weeks before, my dad had asked me to take care of her. He was tired. Not just physically, but emotionally. Tired of being sick. Tired of dragging us through it with him. I gave him my word.

I followed through. I took over everything. I pushed my grief to the side. The funeral happened on a Monday. I returned to work the next day.

By Friday, my boss pulled me into his office. He said I had been doing personal things on company time and reminded me they had allowed me to take Monday off. His words landed like a slap. I stood there silent, humiliated. I made it through a few more weeks before I walked out for good.

That job required more than I had to give. I wasn't ready for the world of deadlines and performance reviews. I returned to waiting tables, picking up freelance gigs, carrying only what I could.

Grief hid beneath years of performance and responsibility. I kept doing. I kept pretending.

Eventually, it surfaced. If you read the chapter on money and the con artist, you already know how that delayed grief shaped my vulnerability. I had no idea how deeply it had followed me until therapy held up a mirror.

I hadn't just avoided grieving my father. I had also skipped over the grief tied to the end of my marriage, the complicated relationship with my mother, and eventually, her death too.

When her health declined, we were estranged. Near the end, my brother called to say she wanted to see me. She was in hospice. I showed up. I also felt relieved that we had done the estate planning. Her will was in place. Her wishes had been documented. That experience shifted something in me.

Planning doesn't guarantee peace, but it creates clarity. Clarity protects the people we leave behind.

Most people don't say it out loud, but it's true. When someone dies without a plan, they leave a mess behind for someone else to clean up. If that person happens to be your child, still grieving and still trying to hold everything together, the damage can run deep. I know. I lived it.

Shock may start at death, but the weight often builds in what follows. The empty chair. The paperwork. The unexpected decisions with no one left to ask. The silence. The expectations. The awkward conversations. The well-meaning phrases that fall flat. "Let me know if you need anything." "My condolences." Those words feel empty when you've lived the loss.

I try to show up differently now. I don't try to fix it. I sit with it. I stay present. Grief is lonely enough. No one should have to go through it without someone willing to meet them where they are.

Death doesn't just mean the loss of a person. It can show up as the end of a marriage, a friendship, a role you once held, or even a pet who was part of your soul. Letting go of Roxy, my 18-year-old shih tzu, broke me in ways I didn't expect. Ending her suffering felt unbearable, even when love required it.

That decision forced me to revisit everything I had learned. Preferences matter. Planning matters. Clarity is one of the kindest gifts we can leave behind.

Improv helped me survive moments like that. There was no script, no cues, no formula for grieving. I had to stay present and keep making the next best choice, even when I had no idea what I was doing.

One of my last performances before my dad passed happened just after I completed improv training at Second City. He came to the show. He called me "Little Miss Hollywood." He was proud. That moment lives permanently in my memory.

Grief never disappeared. The weight stayed, but I learned how to carry it with steadier hands. Peace never came from closure. Only from acceptance.

Improv taught me that control is never the goal. Response matters more. Even in the middle of loss, the next move still belongs to us.

Most people never make that move. Conversations about death get avoided. Plans get delayed. Research reveals the prevalence of avoidance and its profound impact on our well-being.

What the Data Doesn't Let Us Ignore

Earlier in the chapter, I examined how infrequently people discuss death or make plans for it. Research reveals just how deeply avoidance takes root.

Silence around death doesn't ease the ache. Suppression only deepens the suffering later. *Psychology Today* reports that suppressed grief often resurfaces later as anxiety, depression, or

233

even physical illness. The National Institute on Aging warns that unprocessed grief can disrupt daily functioning for months or even years, especially in the absence of a support system.

Avoidance may feel like protection in the moment, but it often leads to more profound emotional consequences later.

Honest conversations about death can ease the emotional load. Harvard Medical School found that people who discuss their wishes with loved ones experience less anxiety, along with greater alignment in care. Stanford's "Letter Project" showed that writing goodbye letters brings closure, clarity, and emotional well-being to both the writer and the recipient.

No amount of readiness softens grief, but intentional planning protects those left behind. Structure emerges in moments that would otherwise feel chaotic, and presence finds space when uncertainty no longer dominates the room.

Death reshapes us in quiet, lasting ways. *The Journal of Death Studies* reports that bereavement often leads to a complete redefinition of self, especially after losing a parent or spouse.

Worldviews shift. Daily routines, belief systems, and identity all begin to realign. The Center for Loss and Life Transition adds that grief does not follow a straight path. It revisits us during milestones, holidays, birthdays, and in quiet, unexpected moments. A song. A smell. A date you forgot you remembered. Grief comes back, not to haunt us, but to remind us that love still lingers.

Grief doesn't just change how we feel. It also reshapes what we believe. The Pew Research Center reports that 60 percent of Americans believe in some form of afterlife. A growing number now identify as spiritual rather than religious. Many people, including those with no formal faith, describe feeling a deep connection to loved ones who have passed.

I have felt it too. Not as a voice or a sign, but as a quiet certainty. Something within me still says, "They're with me." Not gone. Just changed.

Research does more than support the stories in this chapter. Data reveals a deeper truth: Everyone will encounter death. How we respond to it emotionally, practically, and spiritually remains a choice.

Grief rarely arrives in one dramatic moment. Most of the time, it unfolds in a series of small, intentional "New Choices" that allow us to face loss with less fear and more presence.

How Improv Helped Me (and Can Help You)

No rehearsal prepared me. Grief came unscripted and demanded attention I didn't know I had. Improv became my anchor in that uncertainty.

When my father died, no instructions appeared. One day, I was selecting a coffin. The next, I was sitting at my desk acting like nothing had changed. I kept moving through heartbreak, paperwork, family tension, and a kind of fatigue I didn't know how to name. I was improvising, moment by moment.

No tool erased the pain. They helped me face it.

Presence Over Numbness

Improv teaches full-body presence, and grief requires the same. When I asked to see my father's body, I wasn't searching for closure; I needed truth. Presence doesn't always look composed.

Sometimes, it shows up in silence, tears, or blank stares. Staying with the moment gave me something real to hold onto.

Flexibility Over Control

Preparation created a false sense of readiness. I had read the books and taken the class, but I still didn't feel prepared. Improv reminded me that control is an illusion. Flexibility became essential. Through funeral planning, family stress, and emotional overwhelm, I made peace with the fact that I could only respond one step at a time.

Truth Over Avoidance

Improv encourages child-like honesty. In the middle of grief, being honest meant saying what no one else wanted to say. I called out the coffin upsell for what it was. I named the hollowness in the words people offered out of habit. Speaking the truth made the experience more bearable. Pretending would have made it worse.

Momentum Over Perfection

Grief slows everything down. Decision-making feels heavy. Improv taught me to choose anyway; one move forward, then another. Leaving a job that minimized my loss was one of those choices. Waiting for the perfect time never worked. Taking the next step kept me from getting stuck.

Support Over Solutions

Improv creates space for others without needing to rescue them. That mindset helped me show up for grieving friends in a more human way. I stopped trying to fix things. I listened. I stayed present. That kind of support became more powerful than anything I could have said.

Improv never softened the loss. The practice gave me something more substantial than relief. It gave me presence, clarity, and permission to keep choosing. Every moment in grief offered a next move, and I kept saying yes.

Grief doesn't decide the final act. Choice does.

Improvising Your Way Through Grief

Grief may be unpredictable, but your response to it doesn't have to be passive. Below are guided actions and reflection questions to help you process loss, prepare intentionally, and cultivate the kind of presence that creates space for healing, even in the midst of heartbreak.

Scene Work:

Take the stage and move from theory to practice with these quick drills to help you catch your defaults, pivot in the moment, and train your brain for change.

- Have the Hard Conversation: Schedule a conversation with a loved one about end-of-life wishes or create/update important documents (will, healthcare directives). Use this as a connection, not fear.

- Honor Someone You've Lost: Write a letter to someone you're grieving, light a candle in their memory, or share a meaningful story about them with someone new.

- Let Yourself Feel It: Set aside time to grieve something you haven't fully processed. Reflect on what comes up and give it space.

Side Coaching:

Before making more choices, pause and check in. The following prompts will help you be honest about what's on autopilot and what needs to change.

- Where are you delaying grief, and what are you afraid will happen if you stop and feel it?

- What does "presence" look like for you in the face of loss?

- What would it mean to grieve not just the person, but the identity or role tied to them?

Script Revision:

Every rehearsal ends with a new line to carry forward. Try this one on and let it guide your next decision:

> *"Even when I cannot control the outcome, I choose how I show up. I honor loss with presence, love, and courage."*

Encore: The Power of Choosing to Face the Inevitable

Death is the final chapter, but avoiding it doesn't stop the story from closing.

For years, I tried to prepare for loss the same way I approached everything else, by studying, organizing, and clinging to control. I took classes, made checklists, and created plans, believing I could somehow outsmart grief. But every list failed. Grief arrived anyway. Silence followed, not just at the funeral, but in the long, hollow moments that came after.

I didn't know how to hold that silence, so I tried to outrun it. I kept moving. I stayed busy. Until one day, the weight I'd been dodging caught up with me, and taught me something I hadn't expected. Endings don't just take something away from us; they also teach. They invite us to speak more honestly, plan more intentionally, feel more fully, and live more urgently.

From my father's passing, to my mother's final moments in hospice, to saying goodbye to my dog Roxy, every loss demanded the same thing: presence, courage, and adaptability.

Improv helped me find those qualities again. It taught me to navigate uncertainty with openness, to trust the moment, to respond with truth, and to stay connected even when I didn't know what came next. Grief, too, deserves that kind of attention.

Some losses mark the end of a person; others mark the end of a version of ourselves. Each one offers a mirror.

Control never brought me peace. Presence did. Love did. Legacy did.

We don't get to choose whether death comes. But we do get to choose how we live before it does in how we show up, how we speak, and how we love.

Choose boldly. Choose presently. Choose again.

Every ending invites a new beginning and a new choice.

Script Notes: Navigating Death Without a Script

Use these scenes of heartbreak, responsibility, and presence to reflect on your own relationship with loss. No perfect answer exists. Only the next honest moment.

1. **Turning Down Dinner, Then Losing the Chance**

Work felt more important than one meal with my parents. Hours later, my father was gone. That night revealed how quickly "later" can vanish. Guilt grows in the spaces where presence was needed most.

2. **Racing From the Shower to the Voicemail**

Hearing my mother's voice on the machine while still dripping wet marked a turning point. That moment ended my childhood. Decision-making stopped waiting for someone else. I had to choose, even under pressure.

3. **Asking for a Wooden Box, Not a Pitch**

The funeral director talked like a salesman: waterproof coffins and premium features. My dad wouldn't have cared about any of that. A plain wooden box honored him more than anything expensive.

4. **Managing Grief Through Paperwork**

I drowned my sorrow in death certificates and financial logistics. My father's final request was to take care of my mom. I did. What I didn't do was care for myself. That mistake cost me years of unprocessed grief.

5. **Walking Away From a Job That Minimized Loss**

After being scolded for grieving, I packed up and left. That decision had nothing to do with drama. It was about choosing dignity over duty. No paycheck is worth trading in your humanity.

6. **Planning My Mother's Goodbye, Despite the Distance**

We weren't close, but I still honored her wishes. Her will was completed, and her dignity stayed intact. That act wasn't about healing a relationship. It was about closing a chapter with clarity.

7. **Saying Goodbye to Roxy, My Ride-or-Die**

Eighteen years of unconditional love came down to one brutal decision. Letting go taught me that love does not always mean holding on. Sometimes it means making the harder choice with tenderness.

8. **Writing My Own Ending, While Still Here**

Loss after loss showed me what chaos looks like when no plan exists. I created my will, outlining my final wishes and naming the person who would act as my representative.

Part Three
The Perpetual Encore

Chapter 17

Choosing Forward

The Stage Is Always Yours

"The curtain never really falls. It just dims for intermission."
— Gina Trimarco Klauder

Remember those skeptical executives from Chapter One? Arms crossed, eye rolls barely concealed, convinced that theater games had no place in their boardroom? By the end of that session, they were leaning in, building ideas together, discovering that "New Choice" wasn't about performing; it was about living differently.

You might have started this book with your own version of skepticism. Maybe you picked it up during a moment of frustration, when the same patterns kept repeating and you needed something, anything, to shift the momentum. Maybe someone handed it to you, and you weren't sure why improvisational theater would matter outside a comedy club.

Here's what I hope you've discovered: this book is about your ability to improvise, because life is improv. Every moment calls for a decision, and every decision is an act of creation. You're not just reacting to life; you're co-authoring it, one new choice at a time.

What You Already Know

You've learned that being stuck isn't a permanent condition; it's just information. When old choices stop working, your brain isn't broken. It's just running outdated software that can be updated, one small pivot at a time.

You've seen how "Yes, And" transforms conversations, relationships, and internal monologues. Instead of fighting reality or waiting for perfect conditions, you can accept what's true and build from there. That's not settling. That's strategic.

You've practiced calling "New Choice" in areas where you thought you had no options: toxic family dynamics, draining careers, financial chaos, health struggles, and even grief. Every chapter revealed the same truth in different clothing: you always have another move available.

Most importantly, you've rewired the story you tell yourself about change, which doesn't require dramatic overhauls or perfect timing. Change happens in the accumulation of small, brave choices made by someone who decided to stop waiting for permission.

The Imperfect Practice

I'll be honest with you. I still catch myself in default patterns. Last week, I said yes to something I didn't want to do because saying no felt uncomfortable. Two days ago, I spent an hour spiraling about a decision instead of just making it. Even writing this book didn't make me immune to the human tendency to overcomplicate simple choices.

The difference now is speed of recovery. I notice faster. I laugh at myself more easily. I call "New Choice" without the drama I used to attach to changing direction. The practice is about becoming someone who doesn't stay stuck, rather than someone who never gets stuck.

That's what this entire framework offers: not perfection, but flexibility. Not certainty, but responsiveness. Not control, but presence.

Your Next Line

What happens now? You close this book and return to your life, which probably looks the same as it did when you started reading. Same job, same relationships, same responsibilities. The difference isn't in your circumstances. It's in your response to them.

You don't need a master plan. You don't need to revolutionize everything at once. You just need to notice the next moment when you have a choice and make it consciously.

Maybe that means speaking up in a meeting instead of staying silent. Maybe it's saying no to a request that would drain you. Maybe it's having the conversation you've been avoiding, or taking the small risk you've been postponing, or simply breathing through a moment of uncertainty instead of rushing to fix it.

The choice doesn't have to be big to be meaningful. It just has to be yours.

The Ripple Effect

Here's something beautiful about this work: your choices don't just change your life. They give other people permission to change theirs.

When you stop tolerating what no longer serves you, you teach others that they can do the same. When you pivot without shame, you show someone else that changing direction is growth, not failure. When you say "Yes, And" to difficult conversations, you model how collaboration can happen even in conflict.

Your willingness to choose differently becomes a quiet invitation for others to do the same. That's how movements begin. Not with grand gestures, but with individuals who decide they're worth their own best choices.

The Ongoing Experiment

Think of the rest of your life as an improvisation. You don't get the script in advance, but you do get to influence the direction of every scene. Sometimes the plot twists will surprise you. Sometimes other actors will throw you curveballs. Sometimes you'll forget your lines entirely.

That's not a bug in the system. That's life being life.

The question isn't whether you'll face uncertainty, because you will. The question is how you'll respond when you do. Will you freeze and wait for someone else to rescue the scene? Or will you stay present, listen for cues, and make your next move with whatever clarity you can muster?

I vote for the second option. Not because it's easier, but because it's how growth happens. In the space between what you expected and what actually shows up, that's where your real choices live.

Your Encore

If this book has done its job, you now have language for something you've always known: you are not a passive participant in your own life. You are the co-star of every scene you're in.

That comes with responsibility and freedom in equal measure. You can't control every variable, but you can always influence the direction. You can't guarantee outcomes, but you can commit to showing up fully. You can't prevent all difficulties, but you can choose how you engage with them.

One choice at a time. One scene at a time. One brave "Yes, And" at a time.

The stage lights aren't dimming. They're just shifting to illuminate your next moment. The audience isn't waiting for perfection. They're waiting for authenticity. For presence. For someone willing to step into the unknown and create something real.

That someone is you.

The Final New Choice

Here's my final invitation: close this book and make one choice differently than you would have yesterday. Not tomorrow when you feel ready. Not next week when you have a plan. Right now, while the ideas are still fresh and the possibility feels real.

Call someone you've been meaning to call. Say something you've been meaning to say. Start something you've been meaning to start. Or simply notice the next small decision you make and choose it with intention instead of habit.

That's your curtain call. That's your standing ovation. That's your proof that everything in these pages was worth reading. Not because you learned it, but because you lived it.

The New Choice Effect is a way of moving through the world, and the world needs people who know how to move. People who stay flexible without losing their center. People who build bridges instead of walls. People who choose courage over comfort, connection over control, growth over safety.

People exactly like you.

The lights are still on. The stage is still yours.

What's your next line?

References

Bandura, A. (1977). *Social learning theory.* Prentice Hall.

Dweck, C. (2006). Mindset: *The new psychology of success.* Random House.

Limb, C. J., & Braun, A. R. (2008). Neural substrates of spontaneous musical performance: An fMRI study of jazz improvisation. *PLoS ONE,* 3(2), e1679.

Norgaard, M. (2014). How jazz musicians improvise: The central role of auditory and motor patterns. *Music Perception,* 31(3), 271-287.

Lazar, S. W., et al. (2005). Meditation experience is associated with increased cortical thickness. *NeuroReport,* 16(17), 1893-1897.

Books and Publications

Boyd, N. (1945). *Handbook of recreational games.* H.T. FitzSimons Company.

Gosnell, D. (2019). *The vacation effect: Using the science of happiness to recharge your life.* HarperCollins.

Spolin, V. (1963). *Improvisation for the theater: A handbook of teaching and directing techniques.* Northwestern University Press.

Brown, B. (2012). *Daring greatly: How the courage to be vulnerable transforms the way we live, love, parent, and lead.* Gotham Books.

Burg, B., & Mann, J. D. (2007). *The go-giver: A little story about a powerful business idea.* Portfolio.

Clear, J. (2018). *Atomic habits: An easy & proven way to build good habits & break bad ones.* Avery.

Duckworth, A. (2016). Grit: *The power of passion and perseverance.* Scribner.

Dweck, C. (2006). Mindset: *The new psychology of success.* Random House.

Goleman, D. (1995). *Emotional intelligence: Why it matters more than IQ.* Bantam Books.

Goldsmith, M., & Reiter, M. (2007). *What got you here won't get you there: How successful people become even more successful.* Hyperion.

Lencioni, P. (2002). *The five dysfunctions of a team: A leadership fable.* Jossey-Bass.

Sinek, S. (2009). *Start with why: How great leaders inspire everyone to take action.* Portfolio.

Organizations and Survey Data

American Psychological Association (2023). Stress and financial concerns statistics.

Barna Group (2016). Parent influence on spiritual worldview study.

Cleveland Clinic (2020). Men's healthcare avoidance survey.

General Social Survey (2022). Religious affiliation and education trends.

Harvard Business Review Analytic Services (2023). Leadership development survey.

Interpersona (2021). Relationship satisfaction and life satisfaction correlation study.

Kaiser Family Foundation (2022). Healthcare access and cost barriers.

McKinsey & Company (2021). Purpose-driven workplace engagement study.

Pew Research Center (2023). Religious landscape and belief trends.

Historical Sources

Hull House records and documentation of Neva Boyd's work (1920s-1940s)

The Second City Training Center historical archives

Players Workshop of The Second City documentation (1971-1989)

ABOUT THE AUTHOR

Gina Trimarco Klauder leads with humor, heart, and a talent for spotting what others miss. Originally from Chicago, she is an Organizational Development Strategist, keynote speaker, sales and leadership trainer, executive coach, and founder of both Carmine Communications and Carolina Improv Company, with over three decades of experience helping organizations break through cultural, operational, and interpersonal barriers.

Gina's approach combines emotional intelligence, improvisational theater, and behavioral science to create leaders people want to follow, teams that trust one another, and workplaces where humans can be themselves. Her expertise spans seven core areas: leadership development, effective communication, team cohesion, conflict resolution, change management, organizational health optimization, and sales strategy.

A graduate of DePaul University with a B.A. in Communications, Gina will complete her master's in organizational leadership from Anderson University in May 2026. She holds a Certificate in Psychology of Leadership from Cornell University and serves as a fractional organizational health strategist for various organizations.

As founder, artistic director, performer, and director at Carolina Improv Company, Gina operates both an improv theater and training school that helps organizations harness the power of play to unlock real learning. Her specialized work includes medical improv training for healthcare practitioners, teaching physicians and nurses to enhance empathy, communication, and patient engagement through improvisational techniques.

An international bestselling author of *Ignite Your Courage*, Gina keynotes conferences and leads workshops that blend leadership insights with practical tools and straight talk. Her work has transformed teams across diverse industries, including staffing, nonprofits, SaaS, higher education, fintech, hospitality, entertainment, commercial banking, real estate, and healthcare organizations.

When she's not helping teams get unstuck, Gina can be found on stage performing improv or at home with her husband, David, and stepson, Chase. She's also the daughter of an Italian American mobster, a story that makes for compelling keynote material and shaped her understanding of survival, reinvention, and the power of choosing differently.

Gina believes that growth occurs when people feel safe to take risks, that laughter accelerates learning, and that every moment presents an opportunity to make a new choice. She lives in South Carolina, where she continues to help individuals and organizations turn "what if" into "what's next."

To learn more about or to work with Gina, visit ***GinaTrimarco.com***

www.ingramcontent.com/pod-product-compliance
Lightning Source LLC
Chambersburg PA
CBHW070640160426
43194CB00009B/1527